THE SEARCH FOR LOVE

A GUIDE TO YOUR RELATIONSHIPS

THE SEARCH FOR LOVE

A GUIDE TO YOUR RELATIONSHIPS

By Tom Crabtree

EBURY PRESS
LONDON

The characters in this book are creations of the author's imagination and are not intended to portray any real person, living or dead.

Published by Ebury Press
National Magazine House
72 Broadwick Street
London W1V 2BP

First impression 1982

ISBN 0 85223 225 X

Illustrations by Ian Dicks
Cover photograph by John Carter
Book design by Maureen Lowbridge

Typeset in Plantin by Technical Editing Services, London
Printed in Great Britain by The Anchor Press Ltd., Tiptree, Essex
and bound by Cambridge University Press

CONTENTS

Who did you say I am?

When I was at school I got a poke in the back from the art master. There was I, having ruled my two-inch squares, having started to colour them red and yellow (among my favourite colours in those days; red still is), when I felt this sharp pain between my shoulder blades. "You," said the art master. "Woodwork."

For the next four years I tried my hand at making toast racks, book troughs, three-legged stools. Most of them were hurled to the back of the room by the woodwork master. "Appalling," he'd say, tossing a toast rack into the middle distance. It dawned on me fairly quickly that (a) what I was doing was no good and (b) I shouldn't have been there in the first place. I mean, I liked art, and I certainly didn't come to school just to be insulted.

This is why, some time later, when I read Plato's *Republic*, I had no difficulty in understanding his parable of the cave. There are these poor blighters in this cave and they can't see each other; all they can see are shadows. Nothing that they see is real, only shadows cast on the far wall by the firelight. If you took one of these wretches outside and pointed to the sun, the sky, real life, he'd probably make straight back to the cave and the darkness and the shadows—to what he was used to.

Pity I hadn't read Plato when I met the woodwork teacher. "There's a real world of sunshine and possible happiness out there, buster," I could have said, as he pointed out that my three-legged stool wobbled. "People need love and acceptance, pal," I could have told him, "not this kind of murky twilight world of constant frustration and rejection." I could have taken him by the hand and led him to the door and said, "There, sweet Fred. The sun. The sky. We'll all put our toast on a plate from now on and sit on chairs. Let's face it, if I want the kind of thing you're dishing out, I can go for a walk and throw myself into the nearest thorn bush."

I said nothing. I just accepted the pain of it all, thought that's how it was, had to be. But as an adult I began to paint, and two pictures were accepted for an exhibition (*Grandmother In A Wind-tunnel* and *Three Witches*—both dealt with The Rigours of Life). Then I stopped painting. I had just wanted to prove something to myself, a quarter of a century after the poke in the back. It was important to me to know that he was wrong.

It was in the woodwork room that I first began to address myself to those two great philosophical questions: *How am I to live my life? How can I be truly myself?* (Also, *what the hell am I doing here?*) The truth is, I failed to act. I should have gone to see the headmaster and said, "I can't take any more." He might well have said, "My dear chap, if it means so much to you, take art. Sorry that you kept your problem to yourself so long." On the other hand he might have yelled, "Back to the bench, you worm! D'you think you're here to enjoy yourself?" Better to have complained and lost than never to have spoken up at all.

Over the next few years I worked towards a philosophy of action. Do it. Today. No more excuses. Look what happened to Hamlet. Thinking, your books, your philosophising are fine, but they're only rehearsal: in the last analysis it's the deed, the act, *what you do about it* that counts. "*J'ose*," I had on my bedroom wall. "I dare."

At this point you might whisper, *Be careful*. Captain Ahab was a man of action and look what happened to him. Exactly. The first girl I ever went to bed with (blonde, German; I can give no more details in order to protect the innocent) hit me in the face with her elbow just as we were climbing between the sheets. It was an accident, but the pain was terrific. "This is heavenly," I said, seeing stars. I lay there with my nose aching. Life's like that. Just as we're settling down to contentment, or ecstacy, we often get the finger in the back, the inadvertent elbow. By some, this is regarded as no bad thing. "If you knew you were going to win all the time there'd be no point in playing," says Geoff, my friend, the Wise One.

"Gotta have a bit of edge in life, 'aven't you?" says my brother. I was out with him in a small boat in a force eight gale. The waves were washing over the bows and the boat was lurching about, bobbing up and down, like Old Charlie at closing time in The Pure Drop. I was clinging to the mast singing *Eternal Father, Strong To Save* when I looked over at my brother. He was attaching a hook to his fishing rod. "Bit of edge," he says. "Bigger hook. I'll show 'em." We got back safely, of course. Maybe, as those scoutmasters are always saying, we do need a bit of a challenge, a bit of excitement now and again just to remind us that we're really alive.

I'd always hoped to have one moment in my life—the sooner the better—when All Would Be Revealed. I remember, one glorious sunny afternoon, going up to a goat in a friend's garden and saying to him, "I'm me." I looked him straight in the eye and said my name and repeated my assertion. I felt terribly excited about the simple fact of my own identity; I felt, in that sunshine, at one with the world, at peace with myself; I wanted to share it with the goat, tethered to a pear tree at the far end of the lawn. To be honest, he wasn't all that interested, he gave me a brief glance and carried on chewing the grass. You'll know the feeling, like when you're really bursting to share, to live, and the person you're with insists on eating crisps and watching television.

My blinding flash didn't last long. The next day, as I recall, it was raining and I felt quite low, though I did manage to run out to the goat before lunch and say, "Excuse me. Who did I say I was?" What you'll find with Cedric, Jenny, and Carol—and all the other people who flit across the stage in this particular theatre—is that they're born curious and puzzled and, mostly, they stay that way. No Amazing Insight, no All Is Obvious. Just groping towards the light.

Blunder or lurch might be better verbs to use than grope. Life seems—often—just a series of blunders. I've had my share, and some days have been worse than others. Last Spring Bank Holiday I rushed upstairs and goosed my wife (in a playful kind of way). Dressed in a white mini-bathrobe, she was bending over the bath to wash her hair with the shower attachment. "Tea in five minutes," I shouted, dashing away downstairs. When I reached the hall my wife had just come in through the front door. But who—? At table I was introduced to her friend who was staying the night. "You haven't met," said my wife. *We have, in a way,* I almost said.

Things like that are always happening to me. When I was in Kenya doing my National Service, I was on patrol one day and bumped into two chaps wearing Army overcoats and officers' caps, and each carrying a rifle. "Morning," I said to them, in a brisk but friendly tone. They fled. My Masai scout pointed out that they were Mau Mau. How on earth was I supposed to know? I've given a whole lecture to the Women's Institute with my flies open and a bit of pink shirt sticking out. I've jumped on a man's back in the supermarket and shouted, "Harry! Long time no see!" It was not, as you'll have guessed, Harry. Life has to be more than a series of blunders. There has to be a meaning somewhere. It's finding it that's the trick.

When my wife taxes me about these social mishaps I tell her, "At the end of our lives, it's the things we haven't done, rather than the things we have, that we regret." I sometimes think that I should have read philosophy at university.

"What about that time you lurched upstairs and got into bed with Carol and Arthur? I *told* you we were sleeping in the study." I conceded that I learned nothing from that, except that Arthur sleeps on the right and has a chest which feels like a wire brush. Life's a bit of a mystery, but I'm sure we can solve it if it doesn't get too painful along the way.

It's pain that prevents us from getting at the truth, and it's pain—acute pain, emotional pain—that makes us grow. If we can face the hurt, the ache, the resentment within us, we can change; if we can face the truth about ourselves, we can grow. It isn't easy to face up to the tricks, the immaturity and the lies within oneself. To do that, one has to be a very brave soldier indeed. But it's worth the fight. What's the point in living your life by proxy, at one distance removed from your real self—a self that you can respect, like, and be relaxed with?

Let's take an example. One lunchtime last week I was talking to a friend in a pub. He'd left his wife a couple of months previously. There were few regrets on either side, no recriminations. He said he'd leave town, visit once a week just to sort the money out, see how things were, look up his pals. All very civilised. They parted on a high note.

When I saw my friend, there was hardly any recognisable note at all. Just a high-pitched noise, a screech. I've never seen him looking so furious. Apparently, he'd seen his wife, with a man, in a café that *they* used to visit together. "Why there?" he asked me. "She *knows* I like that place; she knows it's special to us. Only an idiot, or someone who was deliberately out to provoke me, would go there so soon after we'd split up." He really was angry. His fists were clenched, his face was white with rage. It seemed a little odd to me that he should be quite *that* annoyed.

"I could wring her neck! I don't care about the bloke; I care about her total lack of feelings. She *knows* I go there. She knows we went there, together."

A fine speech, said with passion. Analysing it, two things need to be said: (a) it was rather thoughtless behaviour on the part of his wife; but (b) what his wife does now that he's left her is no business of his. They are no longer a pair. He has no right to interfere in her affairs. That's what I figured. I also figure that this is another case where strong emotions came in through the door and Sweet Reason vanished through the window.

What I wanted to say to him, as he came back from the bar with yet another drink, was, "Look. The enemy's not out there. It's within you. The enemy is the jealousy and the thought that your ex-partner can exist, live her life, even be happy, without you. Now she's writing her own script; she's no longer dependent upon you. You'd like to be in control, pulling the strings, making her dance when you want her to dance. You can't do that. You have to let go of her, solve your own problems, grow. Let her be. Concentrate on yourself."

I said nothing. He wasn't ready for it, he was too angry, too bewildered. I'll tell him soon, though, as a friend. It's important for him to know. We have to learn to take responsibility for *ourselves*; we have to learn to let other people go, live *their* lives; we have to learn that when people like me write about destructive emotions it isn't a joke. They really can destroy us.

When Cedric split up from his wife ten years ago, there was no animosity. "He wants a mother, a good mother. I don't want to be his mother, I want to be his wife—but he refuses to grow up." That's what his wife told me, after the break. She still sees him occasionally, keeps in touch. She just wanted something different, that's all. I was very sad when that particular partnership ended—not as sad as Cedric, though. It really hurt him. The curious thing is that, having discussed it all for hours on end with me, and with his wife (before the separation), he is still searching for a mother, and not necessarily a good mother—often it's someone who will hurt him, just as his own mother did. We're supposed to learn from experience, but not all of us do.

If you asked me for a word to describe the story of most people's lives, I'd choose "under-achievement". Cedric would be a marvellous person if he could get himself together (most of us would be), but all he can do is make things fall apart. Carol, who searches desperately for the other person, the other half of the torn piece of paper which will make her complete, is married to Arthur, who stays a frog no matter how many times she kisses him. Jenny just wants something that is hers alone; she doesn't want to be spied on or monitored, day in, day out, by the needs and wishes of other people. I know how she feels. I've promised not to tread on her dreams if she won't tread on mine.

Everyone I know is an under-achiever in something. The wealthy ones don't seem to score too highly on happiness and contentment. The intellectuals don't seem all that bright when it comes to the emotions, when it comes to knowing about joy, ecstasy, love and tenderness. The successful ones don't seem to have a lot of fun (they're too busy climbing to the next rung on the ladder).

I'm a great believer in fun. Many British people have the curious, Calvinist notion that you'll never get to Heaven if you laugh too much. The snag is that Heaven may not be Up There, it may be in your heart; you'll miss it all, being miserable while you wait for Heaven. Happiness is catching, so's misery. I once spent a day with a student who used a wheelchair. I can't remember what we talked about as I pushed her about the campus, as we chatted over lunch. I can only remember that she had the most tremendous sense of fun. I felt quite depressed as I went home on the train and looked at the miserable faces of the able-bodied people surrounding me.

Just a word about happiness. It's what most people want, but I doubt whether any of us achieves very much by desperately pursuing it. Happiness is a sort of bonus; it sneaks up on you while you're creating something worthwhile, doing something for other people. I once gave a talk to a school PTA in which I said the aim of education was to teach children how to be happy. The headmaster of the school wasn't too pleased about that. "We're here to help others," he said to me, critically, after the talk. I still think I was right. The quality of your life and your happiness are more important to you than anything else. I'm not saying I know how to catch the bluebird. I am saying that from a very early age we ought seriously to discuss the notion of how to achieve the happiness, the inner harmony, that we all crave.

I'm worried that too many of us may be enlisted into that vast army of emotional under-achievers who, when they try to conduct the mixture of feelings in their own hearts, get a funny, rasping noise instead of a symphony. With some people it's as though the band is perpetually tuning up, never actually getting round to playing a recognisable song. Despite this, *I don't believe that there is anybody who cannot achieve his or her full potential emotionally.* We have a choice. We don't have to settle for the emotional second-rate; we don't have to ignore the voice of our secret hearts; we don't have to be anything less than real.

It's up to you. The colours are all there, in the paintbox of your personality. You have to decide what kind of self-portrait you're going to paint. It may be vivid, alive, using lots of colours; it may be grey, understated, using only a limited selection of hues. How you paint (your style) and what you paint (your subject) are your choice. I can't come along and paint the picture of your life for you. I won't (cross my heart) come up behind you while you're painting, poke you in the back, and say, "You. Woodwork." I respect that what you're doing, however humble the product might appear to an outsider, means a great deal to you. Maybe you're a Rembrandt, and I'm a Picasso. We can't say that you're better than I, nor should we say you're worse—only different. We have to learn to respect that difference, that individuality.

I'm always a bit doubtful about telling anybody what to do. When I was a boy, a friend was always telling me that the answer to a pursuing crocodile was a three-foot stick thrust in its open mouth. That's good advice if you live in a crocodile-infested swamp. If you live in Clapham, it may be better to make sure you're not hit by a bus—and just to be on the safe side, be sure to keep your underwear up to scratch.

I remember, too, as a boy, reading a scouting manual. Ordinary people, it said, sit like this (picture of person slouching in chair); boy scouts sit like this (BS in chair, sitting up straight). For months after that I sat up straight—even on the toilet—with no discernible change in my basic personality. It was then I realised that getting real insight into yourself, changing your values, becoming more truly the person you are, isn't a five-minute business: it's something that takes place step by step and needs determination and guts. It's not easy to change, to grow, but it's worth the effort. Emotional growth makes the difference between existing and living.

Things to think about

○ *Where is the dance before it is danced, the song before it is sung?* It is inside *you.* Sometimes you must dance your dance and sing your song. What is the point of living your life, if at the end of it you say that you never danced, never sang, never had any fun?

○ *There is no one truth, no one universally accepted system of values.* You must choose from those values which collide within you. You may, for example, have to choose between being free and being safe. The choice is yours, nobody else's.

○ *There is, always has been, and always will be a conflict between the needs of the individual and the needs of society.* Your needs may conflict with those who are nearest to you, those you love (every mother knows this). Do you sacrifice yourself for others? If you're a saint, perhaps. If not, I'd say that to lose sight of your own self, your own uniqueness, and your own dreams can be a very dangerous business. You could come out of it not a heroine or hero but a martyr, a depressive, and a walking apology for a real person.

○ *Acknowledge your own history.* George Santayana said that those who cannot remember the past are condemned to fulfil it. Admit your past blunders. Live your life as though it were the only thing that really mattered to you, the Big Picture, a potential emotional masterpiece which is *desperately* important. It is, you know.

○ *Care about what sort of job you're making of your life.* If you're making a mess of it at present, then you're not alone. We can learn from each other.

Getting to know yourself

"Oh, what a face. A noble face. You're probably the most handsome man I've ever seen." Cedric turned away from the mirror. "What do you think of my face?" he asked. I told him that the first signs of madness are that you start talking to yourself and then you get these tiny black hairs growing in the palms of your hands. When people fish for compliments, they may land whoppers.

Cedric is not quite as confident about himself as he appears. Are any of us? For one thing, I saw him glance down at his hands as I spoke, and that business about talking to yourself is, of course, nonsense; I do it all the time. Cedric is slightly barmy, by which I mean that he doesn't abide by convention, the social norms. I think that's why I like him.

"Where id was," said the Godfather (S Freud), "there shall be ego." Siggi wanted to free men (and women) from the chains of their illusions; he wanted us to have insight into ourselves, to understand the world of our unconscious. He claimed that psychic processes are strictly determined (we do as we do because we must), our actions are unconsciously motivated, and these motivations are emotional, rather than rational.

I'll drink to most of that. It isn't only the evidence of dreams or hypnosis, forgetting dental appointments and slips of the tongue ("I'm so glad to hear you've broken your—er, I mean . . .") that convinces me of the existence of the unconscious mind; I can see it in the lives of friends. He marries (four times, to date) the most unsuitable women, for him; she—intelligent, lively, lovely—is married to a drab, impassive husband, remarkably like her own father, not to mention a barrel of lard; Cedric runs after women who will eventually reject him. If it's pain he's after, why doesn't he hit himself over the head with a baseball bat?

A woman I know married a man who used to beat her up. Then she married a man whom she abused emotionally. Now she's entangled with a man who is rude, aggressive, sometimes violent. "Why don't you find yourself a man you actually like?" I've asked her, but I know the answer. She's living out some unconscious drama dating from her childhood. She can't live without conflict, pain, rejection. It's an expensive game.

You can't get self-respect by playing conscious or unconscious charades with other people. You can only get it through people really loving you and telling you so, or by achieving something of which you are proud. Obviously, the more we're loved, the more we love ourselves, and the less we need to manipulate, play games with, or gain power over others. There's a great shortage of love in our society. That's strange, because love is free. By the amount of it about, you'd think it was rationed. I wish we could bottle it and send a few crates to those that need it the most.

Cedric—let's get back to him for a moment—always reminds me of that little boy, Max, in Maurice Sendak's *Where the Wild Things Are.* Cedric, like Max, has in his dreams visited the place where the wild things are. Unlike Max, Cedric hasn't managed to tame his WTs by looking them straight in the eye and telling them, "Be still." With Cedric the WTs roar their terrible roars even louder, gnash their terrible teeth even harder. There's no bowl of soup from mummy at the end of the adventure. Instead, there's chaos and Cedric with his heart broken again.

I've told Cedric he should grow up, stop chasing rainbows, or The Good Mother, and just treat people as potential friends rather than using them to live out his fantasies. I've told him about Freud.

"Who the hell is Freud?" asks Cedric. "Didn't he wet his trousers as a boy? Didn't he have five sisters? No wonder he never said much, just sat there listening. Besides, I reckon Freud was wrong about the id and all that crap. Without emotions people are as rats. Our feelings distinguish us from the apes. Freud—yuck! Didn't he do his first research on how to tell male eels from female eels? How *useless*," he sneered. "Yes, but not to eels," I said, just to have the last word. Cedric wears you out once he starts.

The id—that vast, unconscious region of the mind—is the source of our creativeness, as well as destructiveness. It's the power-house, the boiler room of the good ship *Me.* We can do nothing without the energy that it supplies, and yet we must learn to harness that energy in order to use it to good effect.

I've got a lot more respect for the power of the id than Cedric has. After all, the point that Freud was making was a valid one: we learn to control the id and channel its energies, or civilisation perishes. On the other hand (and this is Cedric's point), if we deny the id, put the lid on it, turn all systems to zero, we are failing to utilise an enormous source of energy within us. We have to learn to look the id straight in the eye, acknowledge that all those nasties are within us, and channel that emotional whoosh into areas which enhance our sense of achievement and our self-respect, rather than into those sombre, destructive areas where we destroy others and ourselves.

For example, I met a woman in a pub. I'd never seen her before in my life. We started talking and after a while she told me, "I hate my husband." I said something about all marriages going through bad patches. "No," she said, calmly. "You don't understand. *Hate.* Like a pure, white light. Like a laser beam. I wake up hating him, I go to bed hating him. If there were hate stories, as well as love stories, I'd be in the Juliet bracket." She paused. "I loathe, hate, despise, totally reject him. I can't stand his physical presence in the same room. When he touches me, I want to curl up and die." Even I was shocked. What a total waste of time and energy! Here was a woman with a passion, all right.

In this kind of off-duty encounter I usually say nothing, taking the line that people must do their own thing without me playing as uninvited psychologist. Yet here was a woman who seemed to be in the process of destroying herself. There are some extremely dangerous fish swimming around in the deep waters of our unconscious minds, including pride, sloth, jealousy, envy, and covetousness, but hate is probably the nastiest customer of the lot.

You can't tell people what to do. They have to decide for themselves. You can say what you honestly think, if they ask you. "What do you think of it all?" she asked me. I discovered she had three children, was in her mid-thirties. "You're young," I said. "You'll spoil your children's lives. Children shouldn't live with hate—nor should you. You'll destroy yourself in the end. Hate eats away at the soul day by day. I hope you want something better for yourself than that." I ordered another drink, finished it, and left. I was quite upset by that little encounter.

Life goes on. There are thousands of people suffering needlessly who make themselves pay a price for something they never did in the first place. I shut away the pain of that woman. How awful, to waste her life like that. Two years later, I was at a party. I was talking in a little group and I felt a hand on my shoulder. I turned around. It was the woman. She looked quite beautiful. Blue blouse, shining eyes, a warm smile: she radiated happiness, the id at its best, in love. "Made it, did you?" I said. "Yes," she said, and kissed me. "Who was that?" somebody asked. "Nobody you know," I said. Nobody I knew, either, but she *was* somebody, a woman of courage, a woman who'd done something positive about living in hatred. Good luck to her, whoever she was.

Jealousy is another all-consuming, negative emotion; it's one that Cedric totally ignores. I don't. I've witnessed its malignant effects, both in my clinic work and among my friends, and I'm struck with nothing less than awe at its power. It destroyed Othello—and Desdemona, killed by his hand—and its track record in ruined lives is quite formidable. You want to gaff jealousy good and proper, before you haul it aboard the *SS Personality.* You could easily lose an arm, a foot; some people have been chewed to death, slowly, by it. A *very* dangerous fish.

A friend told me recently, over a drink, "If my wife slept with anybody else, I'd kill her. No fuss. Just get a knife, kill her, phone the police. I'd have no remorse. I couldn't take it—her being unfaithful." Why do people tell me these awful things? You, buster, have no right to kill her: it's *her* body, *her* life. If she chooses to be faithful to you (and, as far as I know, she is; she loves him deeply), that's *her* business. His wife is a mother-figure to him. The idea of "mummy" sleeping with another man—"rejecting" him, giving somebody else physical love—is totally unbearable to him. It's unfair, primitive, stupid, and irrational, and it could mean a lot of trouble. Indeed. That's the point about getting insight into the nature of your own feelings, your own id. Unless you do, you can't orchestrate your inner music, get the id, ego and super-ego to play in harmony. Instead, you'll be left at the mercy of the more destructive elements within your unconscious mind.

These irrational elements are the lumps in the custard of such sweet-tasting notions as Open Marriage, a Loving Friendship and Doing Your Own Thing. I've known of marriages where one partner has started an affair, even brought the Loved One into the domestic-bliss bit. It's worked—sometimes. More often, all emotional hell has broken loose. "It's either me or that bloody prostitute," one wife said to me, a few weeks after her husband started an open affair with a fairly nondescript and somewhat blue-stockinged girl at the office.

We can be jealous of other people being happy and the only protection we have against that is to be happy ourselves, live in unison with our own inner being, be autonomous and loving individuals. It's not always easy. "I'm not at all jealous," people tell me. Perhaps you mean that you haven't yet met the situation that will evoke all the horrible, mad, destructive feelings within you; you haven't yet met the Big Fish. He's there, forty fathoms down, swimming around in us all. He's an impressive sight when he comes to the surface. Makes Jaws look like a minnow.

Even if we forget Freud (Cedric's *bête noire*) and turn to Jung, the message is the same: *the different parts of the mind must work in harmony.* When they do, you feel alive, invigorated. When they don't, when they're at war with each other, when one part dominates and the others can't get a look-in, you feel lost, debilitated, depressed. You conduct that orchestra within your own mind. How do you get it to play a good tune? What prevents you achieving really heavenly music within your own soul?

Jung's scheme of the mind is similar to Freud's in many ways, but the goodies and nasties are called by different names and the whole tone of the thing is more positive, hopeful and optimistic. With Jung, we have some hope of living our lives as black, shiny-coated retrievers, panting to bring back the bluebird of happiness, rather than—as I sometimes think with Freud—undignified, isolated, whining mongrels tied to the gate-post of our early experience. Freud was *deterministic:* the emotional crop is sown in childhood, all we do is slowly reap the harvest. Jung was *teleological;* he believed that our behaviour is affected by our future aims, as well as our past. I'll drink to Jung on this one.

Let's start with Jung's term of the *persona,* or the mask we present to the world. Your persona is the person you wish others to see: the efficient Super Mum, the successful businesswoman, the elegant hostess, the truly lovely person. For men, it is that charming, witty, handsome man we'd like to project to a breathless world—somewhat like Franz Hals' *Laughing Cavalier* without the silly hat. Sometimes when I go into London I'm eager to project this dashing image, only to hear people whisper, "He's like Oliver Hardy," or worse, "I thought he'd be taller." There's not a lot you can do about height except wear built-up shoes or, like Freud, stand on a box when you have a group photograph taken.

At one time I used to wear grey suits and white shirts to give myself a professional image. "We each have a role to play," I'd tell my wife. "To gain acceptance we must stick to it." Now I bother less about roles and creating the right impression. I try to be myself, all the time. It isn't easy. People expect me to be humorous, devilishly handsome, a sort of Noel Coward with hair. I'm not any of those things—I'm *me.* There are great dangers in playing a part all the time: you are never yourself, you never take a chance that people will like you as you are. The chances are they will. At least, you'd have the satisfaction of knowing that they liked a real person.

When the part we play swamps the real person within us, we run into trouble. We all know what happened to Marilyn Monroe. She created a sex goddess, living out the fantasy that others had constructed for her, lost touch with reality, with her inner being, and paid the price. In Arthur Miller's *Death of A Salesman*, Willy Loman's role as super-salesman so dominates his life that he forgets who he is, was, or could be. He is destined for tragedy as the kite of his persona flies, detached from the solid ground of his true self. We have to try to be the best self we can possibly be, but we don't always do this by living the role that others allot us. Was it Voltaire who said that it's a pity to be born a man and die a grocer? It's a pity, certainly, to be born a woman and die a housewife or worn-out grandmother. Where's the *you* in all this? What happened to all those things *you* wanted to do? Do you use others as an excuse for not daring to try?

When you have the courage to be yourself, come hell or high water, you give others a chance to know you better and to like you *more.* We all suffer from a failure of courage, a reluctance to say, "I'm me." Big bust, tiny bust, thin legs, fat legs, awful hips, grotty feet, gigantic bum—what does it matter? While we're worrying about *that*, life and other people are passing us by. Be real. Using your persona is understandable when you're nervous or in a new situation, but not all the time. If you act all the time, that's cheating. It gives nobody, least of all yourself, a chance to like *you.*

Like Freud, Carl Jung acknowledges the darker, more primitive side of the human personality. Jung calls this shadier, unconscious region of the mind the *shadow.* It contains our instincts, our emotional energy, our animal spirits. Like the id, it is a force for evil, or for good. It has to be channelled. If it is totally suppressed, we lose our spontaneity, creativity, strong insights, joyousness, wisdom, passion. When the self accepts the shadow and is no longer frightened by it, then the personality becomes more alive and vigorous, both mentally and physically.

It is from *dreams*, says Jung, that we gain insight into our inner life, and into our persona and shadow. The dream content, presented in a vivid, encapsulated way, rather like a cartoon, is a comment from the unconscious about our present situation in life.

Some dreams may be a series of unconnected images—the result of eating too much cheese. Other dreams, especially if they occur more than once, could be trying to tell us something urgent. I believe in dreams, whether sleeping or waking.

I had two dreams on successive nights a few years ago. In the first I was a statue in a museum. I stood in a uniform bedecked with medals, alongside Hitler, Mussolini, Goering and other anti-heroes of World War II. In the second dream I was carrying a parcel and being chased by a mob along a cobbled street in, curiously, Mousehole, Cornwall. My pursuers caught me and made me open the package. Inside was something almost worthless: a plastic rain-hat.

I've told you about the grey suits and white shirts I used to wear, the perfect (too perfect?) image that I presented to the world. I won't say that I totally altered my lifestyle because of those dreams, but I recognised that I was unhappy and that I had to do something about it. This situation, which often occurs around the forty mark (especially to men) is called by Jung "coming to a standstill" or "getting stuck". It's the theme of all those fairy stories with a locked door, to which the heroine (or hero) must find a key in order to enter the enchanted garden.

I packed in my job, bought some new clothes (including two-toned shoes), and started to write, which I'd always wanted to do. I've never regretted that decision, financially dangerous though it was. The dreams pointed out something I already knew, deep down. I was up a blind alley, chasing a higher salary, seeking the adulation of colleagues (themselves insecure), building up an ever-more-impressive cardboard cut-out. For once, I had to be true to myself. That's what both dreams were saying.

I'm not suggesting that you buy a caftan and take to the hills. (Phew, you say, that's good. What about the PTA meeting next Thursday?) I'm merely pointing out that your unconscious mind is *not* a cesspool, the repository of all your nasties. I'm saying that sometimes you have to follow your instincts, follow your nose and live your life in harmony with yourself. In dreams, the unconscious mind may tell us the truth, saving us from an emotional wasteland where each part of the personality is at war with the other—where, if we told the truth about ourselves, we could only say, "Whatever I was meant to do, it wasn't this." Life's too short to spend storing up regrets.

In each of our minds, according to Jung, the unconscious areas are the link with that gigantic reservoir of human experience called the *collective unconscious*. In 1906 Jung had a patient who drew some "meaningless" symbols for him. Four years later, an Egyptian papyrus was discovered, and on it were exactly the same symbols that the man, who knew nothing of ancient Egypt, had written. How could he have known anything of this esoteric language, these archaic symbols? Jung explains it by suggesting that the collective unconscious is the sea-bed from which our individual islands of consciousness arise: a substratum common to people from different times and cultures.

Within the collective unconscious there are certain primordial images that we carry about with us. These are the principal actors on a stage which we can never perceive, the *archetypes*, or images, of the different stock characters in human experience. The archetypes include the Witch, the Mother, the Good Fairy, the Father, the Devil. Also present are the *anima*, a man's image of a woman, and the *animus*, a woman's image of a man.

In order to become real people, women must accept and assimilate the animus (ie, masculine components) within them; men must incorporate the anima (the more feminine side of their natures). When a man is able to give love, to feel love, to be gentle, he is truly a man. Women must accept the masculine components within them or they become false, shallow, candy-floss females or (just as bad) belligerent, aggressive females, untrue (as are those "cake-icing" women) to their own natures.

When a man is in love with, or married to a woman, he may project the anima within himself on to her. She is for him not a real person but the Wise Woman, the Good Breast, the Earth Mother, the Provider, the She Wolf, or the Witch. A woman may project the animus within her on to a man: he becomes for her the Wise Man, the Strong Man, the Sick Man, the Child, the Saint, or the Devil. Within every man there is a woman; in every woman, a man. The most successful partnerships are those in which the woman's animus and the man's anima are not repressed and in which strict roles of "masculine" and "feminine" are not adhered to. The royal road to friendship is to treat your partner as a real person (not as easy as it sounds with all those figures strolling about in the unconscious) and to have flexibility of roles. Nothing is more boring than the macho man unless it's the candy-floss lady.

I must admit at this point that I disagree with Carl Jung about one thing. Carl had this theory of *psychological types* and was keen to divide the world into *introverts* and *extroverts*. This won't wash. Most of us are a mixture of both; a great deal depends on whom we are with and what day of the week it is. I once took a personality test and came out of it a "neurotic extrovert". Little Noddy might be, but not me. Monday mornings, I'm a neurotic introvert; by Friday afternoon, I'm a stable, outgoing extrovert: a more pleasant sort of person you couldn't wish to meet. Whatever I am, I am—like you—a unique individual. Tidy up the world if you must, Carl, but don't label me, put me in a drawer. To be fair, CJ himself writes, "It was one of the greatest experiences of my life to discover how enormously different people's psyches are." That's true, and although it's a problem for psychology as a science, it makes life a great deal more interesting. The fact is that you and I are one-offs.

Jung gives a place in his theories to the irrational, mystic side of life. Jung travelled abroad extensively to study the customs and behaviour of primitive tribes. He was impressed by their wisdom. Primitive people are close to the earth. They have an affinity with the moon, the sun, and the ocean. They are closer to their god. It is primitive people, says Jung, who grow old peacefully. They know that life has a natural cycle; they do not neurotically pursue eternal youth, for they know that every life has a morning, an afternoon and an evening, and that what was true in the morning will by evening have become a lie.

When the customs of primitive culture are examined closely they make sense. If a Pueblo Indian doesn't feel in the right mood, he stays away from the council. When an ancient Roman stumbled on the threshold as he left his house, he gave up his plans for the day. I go along with that. If it's one of those days, I do as little as possible. What's the point if the fates are against you temporarily? That's silly, you say, just a lot of superstition. But with the Pueblo Indian it wasn't. When he wasn't at his best, a rattlesnake got him; no doubt, nasty things happened to the Ancient Roman on an off day, too. Everything going wrong? Stay in. Do nowt. It makes sense.

Primitive folk believe that everything is spirit. I'll drink to that. What about a chair? you ask. All you can do is argue it out with a nuclear physicist. Primitive folk believe that great art comes from God; some people are merely tuned in to the right waveband to pick up the transmission. I'll buy that, too. Primitive people observe that there is a power in life greater than themselves; they avoid the cosmic arrogance, the lack of reverence for nature that besets Western civilisation. I doubt whether we can afford to dispense with the spirituality that motivates "primitives". As for irrationality, all I can say is, take a look around you. I'm surrounded by educated but irrational people.

What I most like about Jung is his attitude towards therapy. He did not, like Freud, set up as the One Who Knows It All, and he was less interested in the past than in the present. Freud saw his patients as being held up by their inability to free themselves from their fixations with the past, but Jung believed that the regression we all show to past fixations results from a block in the present.

At one time, I was with Freud in this. I used to sit in my consulting room in my best suit and Chinese-laundered shirts, murmuring "Mm, hm," and, after some weeks, "Tell me about your childhood." This is known to me as the Method Acting, out of

Stanislavsky, School of Therapy. The idea was that you unravelled the knots in the patient's psychic ball of wool as you sat there half-asleep. Very restful, this catatonic approach, but the snag is that it helps the therapist more than the patient. What the patient wants is not speculation about her infancy, but a key to open the locked door, or another exit so that she can get out of the jam she is in. In particular, if she feels that life has no meaning, she wants someone who will sympathise, but also tell her that life can be beautiful, and that it is shot through with potential meaning. She doesn't want Freud's obsession with the body.

I've learned a couple of things about therapy in my time at it. The first is that if the patient likes you, he or she gains hope, grows in confidence and gets better! The second thing is that nobody knows how therapy works, and it doesn't happen only in clinics but is going on everywhere: in the offices, in pubs, in the kitchen, anywhere human beings get together and talk to each other. The therapist is just a person who helps with the process of conquering pain and self-doubt. I've met men and women who, though untrained, were much better therapists than I'll ever be.

Freud died of cancer, a sceptic to the last. Jung died with an all-abiding belief in God and in the holy spirit that resides within each and every human being. *That*, in the face of his own Swiss pastor father's loss of faith, was his triumph. His other victory was in who he was. If I'd met Jung, I'm sure that I would have liked him. Not so of Freud; he would have made me feel quite depressed.

Let's take a quick look at the ideas of Alfred Adler, and especially his notion that the antidote to neurosis is *Gemeinschaftgefühl*, community feeling. Freud's criteria for mental health were to be able to work, and to love. Adler includes a third: the ability to form friendships. To avoid neurosis, says Alfred, we must learn to substitute shared, social goals for selfish, individual goals. Freud emphasised the past; Jung emphasised the future. Freud emphasised loneliness, the intra-psychic war with individuals fighting alone against the incessant demands of the id. Adler reminds us that people live in *groups* and it is in working co-operatively with others in *social relationships* that many of us find solace and therapy, not to mention happiness, self-respect and purpose. None of us should spend a whole lifetime looking in the mirror.

I think Adler's right about this. The group is terribly important to human beings. Men and women are social animals; few of us can be happy alone. Working in a clinic with depressed mothers, particularly those shut up in a house all day with young children, my first thought was: is there any group this mother could join which would get her away from four walls and take her "out of herself"? Alone, our problems are magnified; with friendship and companionship we begin to see other people have problems, too. We begin to get our own difficulties into perspective.

When I look back on my clinic work, I can see that manipulating human situations (urging mum to find a part-time job, to help out at a playgroup, or to do some voluntary work; urging dad to do a bit more around the house, to build up a relationship with his own children) rather than poking about in the id often brought the best results. The aim was to strengthen the ego and boost the person's self-respect; this was the bulwark against the intrusions of the id and against depression. Who did the therapy? Not me. Most of it was done in the group, by people talking, listening, working alongside each other.

The healing power of friendship, learning to work for and alongside others, offers the best remedy for conflict and neurosis. Diagnosis is not cure. What's the point in labelling this mother depressed, that father neurotic? It's what we *do* about it that counts. It is in the group, within the community, that the best therapy is available: not in the clinic, being interminably analysed, giving fancy names to what is most of the time old-fashioned loneliness or unhappiness. The cure for "dis-ease", according to Adler, lies not in unravelling the ball of wool of one's early complexes, but rather in substituting new, more socially oriented goals in place of self-obsession, self-aggrandisement.

Adler used to ask his patients: "What would you do if you could walk out of here fit and well?" Most of the time it was the patient's neurotic lifestyle which was the *cause* of the dis-ease: striving for spurious goals, always attempting to compensate for some imagined inferiority. "To be a human being," wrote Adler, "means the possession of a feeling of inferiority that is constantly pressing on towards its own conquest."

Look in the mirror, and you'll see what Adler meant. I don't expect that, like Cedric, you'll leap about with delight at your own appearance, but I hope that you won't feel dismayed either. Your individuality is all you have. That's you. You have to accept and like yourself. If you don't, how can you expect others to accept you? Look at the others and what do you see? People who are confused, even miserable, just like you. People not sure of themselves, shy, prone to bouts of self-doubt and depression, just like you. People who get angry, people who feel frustrated, sad, utterly dejected, just like you. People who are capable—given human sympathy and a little understanding—of happiness, joy and ecstasy. Human beings, *just like you.*

Poor Siggi Freud. Is Cedric right about that? Wet trousers and never spoke to his sisters or brother? No wonder he saw it as a dangerous, lonely world.

Tips towards self-fulfilment

○ *Learn to accept yourself: bad habits, good bits.* "You" is all you have.

○ *Not too much self-analysis and psychology.* Life is about people, relationships. Reach out, rather than looking inwards.

○ *Only connect.* No man, or woman, is an island. We exist inasmuch as we relate to others. Adler knew that. With a face like Miss Piggy, except in the dusk with the light behind him, he hadn't got an awful lot going for him, appearance-wise. Probably far less than you. Adler liked people—that counts for a lot.

○ *Don't assume that other people are perfect, haven't got doubts, tribulations, their own crosses to bear.* That attractive man over there, this well-dressed woman over here, are just as lonely, afraid, unsure of themselves as you or I.

○ *To understand yourself is to accept your own humanity and the humanity of others.* Accept the naughty bits in your unconscious; don't poke about in there; don't put yourself down. I'm not much to look at. I'll take my chances with the rest of you. Alone, we're done for. Together, we'll make out.

○ *Sometimes, just once in a while, follow your star, follow your dream, trust your instincts.* Your unconscious mind can be a trouble-maker, I know; it can also be a great source of wisdom.

○ *Don't keep the lid on the id, not all the time.* Give your id a day out occasionally. Do something spectacularly crazy and romantic once a month, just to prove to yourself that—although life is serious—it was never meant to be totally grey and dreary.

○ *You have as much right to be happy as anybody else.* Don't wallow in misery, self-doubt, self-inflicted pain (see chapter 8 on guilt for more about this kind of thing). You belong on this earth and should feel at home in it. You have only one life—don't waste it.

○ *The best defence against the destructive elements within the id is self-respect; a healthy Self-Regarding Sentiment.* You can only get this by achieving something of which you are justly proud—whether it's climbing a mountain or baking a Black Forest gâteau—or by other people telling you that they love/like/respect you. This has to be worked for. Don't be lazy, especially about love.

○ *Be real.* Why pretend? The real you is better than most people deserve. They're lucky to have you. They're unlucky if you give them Florence Nightingale, Sigmund Freud or some other person you've drummed up that's not you at all. To hell with people who don't like you as you are. Think what they're missing. You are unique. Honestly.

I'm me—but what about the others?

Just a minute, you say. All that stuff about being true to yourself, never pretending, being real. Buddy, I'd love to be real (this is you talking) if somebody would only whisper in my left ear which of the masks I wear is The Real Me. A woman in her time plays many parts: innocent maiden, reliable employee, companion, seductress, charming hostess, lover, housewife, skivvy, vamp, sex object, cook. Which among that lot is ME? Don't get shirty. I can see the problem. I still don't believe that each one of us is a Cast of Thousands, wearing the right clothes, saying the right things, according to which play we happen to be in. Sometimes we do have to pretend. I'll concede *that*. I still believe that underneath all the role-playing is a real you.

Prove it, buster, you say. I'm not sure I can. There's the you when you're in love with someone who loves you; then you don't have to pretend. There's the you when you're with old friends, when acting, subterfuge and putting on airs and graces are (or should be) unnecessary. Aha, you say, but then I just don the mask of Old Friend from my vast repertoire of possible selves, and go in for the nostalgia bit. In fact, everywhere I go I act the appropriate part according to the situation I'm in, the people I'm with, and I try to put on the best show I can. I suspect that behind all my masks is a vast space, a void—not a Real Me at all.

I know the problem. A psychiatrist once told me that in America he met a high-powered executive who started to describe the demands of his job, the power he had, the hectic schedules he had to meet. Said the shrink, "That's all very well, but where is the *real* you?" The HPE thought for a full minute, then said, "My Real Self pushed off years ago and I haven't seen him since." We all know people like that, chameleon personalities who change with their surroundings. Like onions, they seem to have layer upon layer of disguises, roles, and they don't have any core, any centre.

All I'm saying is that within each of us there is a True Self, which admittedly still has to be confirmed by others. If we lose touch with that true self we feel disoriented, ill at ease, unhappy. We can live with a false self some of the time, but not all of the time. If family, workmates, friends insist upon us presenting a false self day in, day out, then we become prone to breakdown, stress—dis-ease.

Sometimes alcohol or anxiety can diminish our social performance and make the mask slip. At one party where I was host, I didn't touch a drop until 11 p.m. Beforehand I was Utterly Lovely, making sure people were enjoying themselves, introducing guests, re-charging glasses. At 11 p.m. I started drinking; by midnight I was tiddly. While in the kitchen, I told a woman, "You have a lovely face. I'm drawn to you as a moth to the flame. I would go through hell just to hold your hand." I put my arm around her. We kissed, the dishes in the sink rattled, trains roared through tunnels. Next day I rang her up to apologise. "I enjoyed it all," she said. "I like you when you're romantic." I'm learning to say what I'm really thinking when I'm sober. It takes time to learn to be that spontaneous, but it's worth it.

Cedric's a lot more spontaneous than I. That lunatic quality—zany, spontaneous, surrealistic—is all there. There's no point in pretending. We know him for the loony he is. "I have a dental appointment on Tuesday at 2.30," he says, one terrible joke after the other. Later, as he plays *In a Shady Nook* on the piano and sings—the eerie call of a pregnant yak is nothing compared with this—he'll start insulting huge, granite-like builders' labourers and say things like, "Watch it, Doris. I stopped Schmelling in three." When they throw him out to cries of "Mind my Sherlock Holmes hat", I expect those navvies to turn on me. "Good laugh, your mate," they say. Curiously, when he's himself Cedric has this charisma; he's forgiven even when he breaks the rules.

Those rules of dress, conversation and behaviour exist to oil the wheels of human interaction. Without them, there'd be chaos; with too much ritual, you don't get a chance to know people really well. Sometimes you don't want to know them; you deliberately keep things at a surface level. But if you do want to get to know them, it can be very annoying when you're foisted off with a lot of meaningless chat. Words can be used to communicate or to prevent communication and set up a verbal smoke screen.

Geoff, the Wise One, hates going to parties. He's developed a whole range of smoke canisters to cope with the verbals. His speciality is psychobabble. "Skinner," he'll say, eating a sausage, "is fine, but it's E V Croup who reflects the *Angst* of our century, the existential *Fingerspitzengefühl* of the *Zeitgeist*." I've seen quite pretty women looking at him in wonder. Little do they know that Evelyn Croup was a woman he met up at the launderette who was worried sick about her weight.

Geoff will explain to a Lovely Woman about operant conditioning and behaviour modification. "My wife," he'll say, "has commenced a new behaviour modification programme with the children." This usually results in eyelashes fluttering, if not a whispered, "God, with a man like this I could conquer the world, even parts of Birkenhead." What Geoff doesn't explain is that when the kids trail mud in from the garden, Elaine chases them with the broom. Geoff wears a badge saying "Groddeck was right". He has another one which reads "Existentialism—now". He relies on words such as "structuralism", "*Gestalt*" and "syntonic" to confuse his protagonists. "For syntony, give me Pissaro," he'll say to some innocent sucking a Twiglet. Few cards can trump that.

The third main tactic Geoff uses is the impressive-sounding, completely isolated fact. This is usually hurled in, like a hand-grenade, if a topic is being discussed which he knows nothing about. "Shakespeare left £10 to the poor of Stratford and the second-best bed to his wife." (That's literature covered.) "Plato means 'chunky'. He was a wrestler." (Ancient history.) "Samos is the best of the Greek islands—the home of Pythagoras." (Holidays.) "Fresh air is the cure for scrofula/bad breath/flat feet." (Medicine. Here, apparently, any pronouncement has to be made in a loud voice.) "Karl Marx had his bumps read by a phrenologist. Chamberlain was also interested in bump reading. When he met Hitler, he ran his hand through Adolph's hair and ruined the Führer's quiff, hence

World War II." (Politics.) "In America they have toilet paper on which there are crossword puzzles." (Life.) At parties Geoff comes over as a well-read, much-travelled man with a fair grasp of anything from archaeology to space travel. As a matter of fact, he's interested in growing flowers, but never talks about flowers at parties; roses, especially, mean far too much to him.

I suppose, with a degree in sociology, Geoff should be able to work out some kind of act, gird himself around with verbal armour. Let's say that we'd *all* worked out a Protective Coating, and let's say that we could always remember people's names. Let's say you've got your social performance polished and that neither anxiety nor alcohol are going to let you down. There's just one thing we've overlooked. You still may have to cope with children.

I took my daughter, then three, to a neighbour's house when I went to borrow a paintbrush. She, confident little madam, marched into their living room and looked around. "Well," she said, "*I* don't think their curtains are terrible." As the man was talking to me, my daughter was looking at his mouth, closely. "My mummy says you've got teeth like Dracula, but *I* don't think you have." By now, I was thinking of using a roller. "There are no toys in this house," said the D, "and your face isn't very white. Huh." She looked at me. I agreed we should go. I wasn't so much disappointed as thinking of something good to say about the carpet. "And this *isn't* like a bloody Christmas grotto," said the D, taking a last look around at the room. It took me weeks to get over that; I explained that my daughter was very imaginative if not positively syntonic.

My advice with regard to conversation is to be as natural as possible, and listen to what the other person is saying rather than wait, straining at the leash, to make some witty, astounding remark once there's a pause. People try too hard. One *has* to bear the initial anxiety of tuning in to each other. Better that than to set up a whole series of false trails and not give anybody the chance to get to know you. I used to know a woman who would have A List of Topics to Talk About; she'd start at the top and work her way down. "How are you?" you'd ask. "I see that petrol's gone up again," she'd reply. People need conversational stroking, to be paid some attention. They want you to think well of them; you want them to think well of you. Let them bat first. They'll like you all the more for not being overly anxious to show that you are unique, a person who's worth knowing.

Remember, though, that words have their limits as a means of conveying intentions. A simple gesture, as every lover knows, can be much more powerful than mere words. In times of tragedy, a hand held, an arm around the shoulder, or a hug can convey more than words ever can.

Words can have a magic potency ("I love you"); they can be terribly sad ("Too late"); they can condense and symbolise a whole area of experience ("Bike Boys Rule"). Human beings are different from other animals in that they have words with which to reflect upon their experiences and structure their worlds. You don't get lions asking each other, "Yes, but what is life *for*?" You don't find ants saying, "All work and no play can't be good news." Words are what make humans different from apes, but I still have my suspicions about them.

When I was sixteen I met a girl of my own age to take her to a party. "Shall we go for a walk instead?" she asked me. I agreed. She took my hand. "Do you like holding hands?" she asked. Do I like holding hands? If I had my way we'd hold hands at bus stops, airports, railway stations; the whole world would hold hands. I've met few women since who've said to me, "Let's miss the dance/dinner/talk on the flora and fauna of the alimentary canal. Let's go for a walk and hold hands." I like good conversation, good food and entertainment in that order. Best of all, I like touch. Ask me to hold your hand in the supermarket, just look into your eyes quietly for five minutes as the world rushes past, and I will. Words are fine, but there are some situations they don't cover.

Let's turn to clothes. Perhaps clothes illustrate better than anything else the on-going problem we have with saying "This is me" to other people. We need other people's affirmation of our own identity. We seek it through symbolic interactions (eg, having a cup of tea together), through words, gestures, and joint enterprises. We also seek it through clothes. We all have an I, or ego—that residue of experiences that remains within us and shapes our personality—but how do we present ourselves to other people? What kind of person do we want others to see? Clothes are to do with the presentation of identity. I know who I am, but how do I get the message across?

Clothes tell the world who we are or would like to be. They may say something about our values, our role in society, our aspirations, or the group we adhere to. The world is a stage: the word personality comes from the Latin *persona*, or mask, and the role we play derives from the Latin *rotula*, the scroll on which the actor's lines were written. Clothes provide warmth, protection, hygiene, decoration, but what is their main purpose? "To dress up in, make us look more attractive," shouts somebody at the back. Good egg. What we're talking about here is not the I—the inner eye—but the *me*, the image that we hope to project.

It's hard to know what kind of impact to go for, especially among strangers or when you're starting a new job. When I give my latest collection of sartorial rejects to the Nearly New Stall at St Ursula's, the nuns always ask, "Haven't found a suitable *persona* yet? Never mind. We can always move stuff for your shorter, rounder man." Good-living, well-read people, those nuns, but cheeky. In my mind's eye I see myself as combining the best of Paul Newman and Robert Redford; when I go to the tailor's I see Oliver Hardy looking back at me out of the mirror. Push off, Fatty, who invited you? I'm hoping for a looking-glass self that will reflect the slim, whipcord-bodied, sensuous man somewhere inside me, but this is more like the Hall of Mirrors. It's this distortion of me, the constant disappointment with my own image, that keeps the Nearly New Stall at St U's one of the best-stocked stalls in the business.

Women, particularly, will sympathise with this dilemma as to what to wear to reflect the Real You. One day it's see-through crocheted dress and black tights to lure that interesting-looking milkman/chap in the office/man at DIY Furniture Restoration. Assume that this has no effect. Will a woman with integrity stop there, say, "He doesn't deserve me"? No. Next day it's jumper, skirt and sensible shoes to see what effect *that* has. I know a woman who carried a riding crop and black hat to work to lure to her bosom a man who was interested in horses. She did, too. Let's hope that she got the requisite burning kisses on upturned face for her pains; a lot of these horsey types can think of no better way to reward a woman than to pat her neck, give her a sugar lump and shout silly things in the bedroom, like "They're off!" What on earth do women see in tall, saturnine-looking men who are terribly rich and own strings of horses? Let's see a lot more short, balding men on those TV advertisements, I say.

In this fast-moving world, the quick impact is vital. If you don't get it right the first time, you may never get another chance. When people lived in villages and you fell in love with, say, Farmer G's eldest son, and he ignored you at the village dance, you could always go back to the cottage, get out a piece of paper and pencil and work out a strategy. You could find out where he was on Saturday nights, knew he'd be in church on Sunday. Now, if you see an incredibly handsome man at the bus stop, you have to move fast. He could be a pilot with Patagonian Airlines, or he could have come from the Isle of Mull. (If you're on Mull, for Mull, read Penzance.) It's no good thinking that you'll see him in church next week and wear your new bonnet. You have to fall against him and say, "I've got something in my eye," and make sure he can't see the hole in your tights.

I remember when Carol was keen on Paul last year. I played gooseberry, meeting the two of them in The Pure Drop every lunchtime. Carol (42-32-44) was dressed in a tight white blouse the first time, and it had a loose button. The thought of all that Rubens' *Rape of the Daughters of Leucippus* flesh bursting out was too much for old Charlie. He stood at the bar hitting the back of his neck with his fist. The white see-through summer dress was a big hit—with the lads in the saloon bar, at least. Paul didn't seem to take much notice.

On Wednesday, it was a tight, knitted, figure-hugging dress. The saloon bar crowd were all in the public by now, invading our space, staring at Carol, spilling their drinks. "Is this dress too blatant?" asked Carol, as Paul went to re-charge the glasses. "The glory of creation is in its infinite variety," I said (many of my best remarks in the PD are borrowed from Captain Kirk of *Star Trek*). By Friday Carol had reverted to a polo-necked sweater and tweed skirt. Old Charlie's hopes of her rising to the ceiling like Botticelli's *Venus* were well and truly dashed (the PD does have those shell ashtrays, not as big as in the painting, though). The saloon bar mob drifted back to their usual haunt.

"What sort of clothes d'you like women to wear then, Paul?" I asked him on the Friday, when Carol was in the loo. "I like long flowered frocks myself," he said. "I think they look extremely feminine." Good God. What a waste of time and effort. Honestly, what women see in thin, six-foot-tall men who talk posh and don't like dresses or blouses that have to be sprayed on I'll never know, especially men like that with lots of hair.

Let's face it. We do create an impression with the clothes we wear; they can amaze, disgust, turn on, switch off, dismay, delight or bore other people. Clothes convey messages. With men, they can indicate status, social class, the fact that one isn't short of a bob or two. Two years ago I was on a train, minding my own business. This man opposite me lifted his left leg, held his foot in his hand. *A yoga freak,* I thought. "See this shoe?" he asked. "How much would you reckon they cost?" I say, where's my *Beano*? Gentlemen don't cock their legs in front of strangers. They were, apparently, £35. Suit, £250. Tie, £20. He told me that he was a "hit man" by profession, travelling to Manchester to "lean on" somebody. I was going to ask him about his underpants, but I thought better of it.

"Never £40, squire," he said, as he got off the train (it was the price that I'd put on his suit, the most outlandish one I could think of; for £40 you could buy out our local annual jumble, and they'd throw in the tea ladies). "Forty, guv?" he said, wrinkling his forehead sadly as he moved off. Sorry, old chap.

Given that clothes can be one of the strategies that we use to gain approval, admiration, or even love, let's ask who do *women* aim to please or impress? One survey found that men dressed to win the approval of women, and women dressed to win the approval of other women. Both men and women thought that appearance was more important when with strangers than with friends and spent hours deliberating on what to wear before that crucial first meeting. First impressions seemed to count a lot.

My own research, conducted on my wife, suggests that what a woman wears depends on whom she is with at the time. When the beautiful Claudine comes to visit us from France, everybody starts looking incredibly smart. Claudine raises the standard. So does my sister with her amazing shoes and dresses. It's back to the wardrobe—jerseys and jeans abandoned—as these two living attributes to sartorial elegance float in from Paris and Southend respectively. "Why don't you keep your fisherman knit on when Claudine comes? What about integrity?" I ask her. "Button it, Woodentop," says my wife. She can be very cutting when she wants to be, even in jeans.

It's the urge to belong to a group that makes many of us heed the dictates of fashion. With my kids, style *c'est l'homme et la femme.* At one time we used to palm them off with my wife's sister's kids' rejects and stuff from the jumble. No more. Clothes are part of the image, an important part of the message that they wish to send out to their peers. We're all in there, conforming, sending out messages. I mean, would you trust your bank manager with your money if he dressed like an ageing hippy? Or your dentist with your teeth if she looked like a Hell's Angel? Roles have to be played. All of us (unless we're terribly rich—or poor) have to conform, play a role, meet the expectations of others.

Still, I don't think that we should conform all the time. Clothes should be fun, they're meant to be enjoyed, so my advice is dare to bring that underlying, sexy you out of purdah. Few men have died of sexual arousal, and those who might would be no good to you anyway. Lure that Heathcliff type in the next chair/office/street to you via a white blouse, black bra and mini, then bind him to you with super-glue lipstick and gesture to him to throw away his brown suit. Be bold, be colourful. You don't have to look all that dependable. Try being Conspicuous Outrage rather than Minnie Mouse. There's only one thing worse than being spoken about behind one's back—being ignored.

Final word about clothes. Undies. I hope you won't let me down if you're hit by a bus. "From the cradle to the coffin," says Bertolt Brecht, in *The Threepenny Opera*, "underwear comes first." No woman shimmering magnificently in over a thousand hand-sewn sequins will, I hope, stoop to tatty knickers. Which of us, on a weekend visit to friends, wishes to see the butler glide away with our dropped drawers on a silver tray? Check elastic. Confident on top, immaculate underneath: that's the form. But, you say, nobody but my partner ever sees my pants. Hardly the point. You'll know you're elegant all through; that makes you feel safer, more secure, even though you live nowhere near a bus route or don't visit country houses with butlers.

Years ago I had a rendezvous with a beautiful girl. We stood on a lonely beach, tearing off our clothes to get at each other. Then she saw my baggy underpants. She laughed so much that she collapsed into the sea foam, fortunately dragging me down with her. "A man with such torn and tattered baggies cannot be other than in need of a great deal of love. Come, my beauty." (I think she'd been reading *Tess of the d'Urbervilles*.) You may not be so lucky. Clean undies, then do your own thing.

In our search for affirmation of identity, our constant yearning for love, there's a difference between how we see ourselves and how we wish others would see us. This is particularly true of sexual attractiveness. Inside we may know that in the SA League we are second, if not third division. We worry because we're too tall/short, because our mouth/bottom is too small/large, because we have big hips/feet/ears. With sex, nobody wants to hear the truth. As Carol says, "God save me from understanding. Give me passion, tell me a few lies!" You could lean over the fence, say to the man next door, "I have a 1-10 scale of male sexual attractiveness. I give you a good three." It may be true. I doubt that he wants to hear it.

With sex, you have to be like a skilled teacher: look for the strengths, build on them. I didn't understand this at one time. I met this woman, Winnie, in the launderette. "Do you keep losing socks?" she asked me. I raised one trouser leg to show her a trim ankle. Our friendship blossomed. I told her about my scale of women's attractiveness (A-E) and said she was a B. (Well, her feet *were* big and her hair was an aesthetic disaster, but both were, strangely, very sexy.) That was the end of the relationship. She, I realise now, wanted to know that in my eyes she was an A plus; she knew the truth, but she figured that unless *I* saw her as an A she should look elsewhere. My advice in sexual relationships is to treat your partner as a remedial case: look for the good, encourage and build on it. "Tell me I'm beautiful again, darling," you could say. "No, women don't have stamen, try a little lower down." With people you meet, tell them that they have a nice face or long eyelashes or shapely finger-nails. Make them believe they're an A. It's no skin off your nose. If you take up with them, never tell them they're C plus. With sex, with love, the only people who really matter will see us as first division material, despite the facts.

Apart from sex, I think the aim is to avoid playing too many games. The kind of game I like is where a beautiful woman says to me, "I'll hide in that big cupboard over there and you have to try to find me." I don't like games in which one person sets up as a psychiatrist/parent/bug exterminator and the other person is expected to be a patient/child/cockroach. Eric Berne, a Canadian-born psychiatrist who practised in San Francisco, tells us of the manifold ways in which people can manipulate each other. Berne described how within each of us there are parent, adult, and child states. Any two of us can relate to each other in any number of ways. We can, for example, play at parent-child or, if we get sick of this, we could play adult-child, or child-child. Every game has its dangers. After all, we're adults and should treat each other as such. Berne expounded the theory that each person plays out a pattern; the pattern is set in childhood and is called a "life-script". Those with winning scripts he called "princes"; those with losing scripts he called "frogs". Berne used to say, "My business is turning frogs into princes." My daughter knows all about this, although she's never heard of Berne. When she tries on yet another dress before going out with her boyfriend, I ask, "Changed again, have you?" Going upstairs, for the sixth time, she says, with feeling, "I'm tired of being a frog."

I must be honest and say that these games of You Be The Mat/I'll Walk All Over You alarm me. They can waste so much time and lead to so much destruction. With some relationships, and especially with some marriages, it's worse than frogs and princes. It's as though one partner had hypnotised the other into doing the most undignified, infantile, degrading things. The star gives his partner a walk-on part in a drama, the script of which *he* has written.

I despise all of this. I like to write my own script, do my own thing as far as possible, and have fun. Life's no good if you never have any fun—and if you never have any say as to what you want from a relationship. Why play a tatty part in somebody else's play? Why settle for the role of canteen orderly in a latter-day Hitler's army? Why play the doctor or patient when you're not even in hospital? There's a whole, wide, beautiful world out there and I'll go part of the way with you, with pleasure and joy, providing that you treat me with courtesy and as an adult (and I promise to do the same with you). We *will* play games. You hide behind that oak tree in the middle of this sun-kissed, tranquil field, I'll count to ten and then I'll try to find you. We'll take it on from there, as adults, human beings—not frogs. If you want to, pretend I'm a prince, you're a princess. You look a definite A to me.

It isn't easy in the ever-changing world in which we live to retain a sense of authenticity, to avoid the alienation, sense of loss and bewilderment that too-large institutions bring to most human beings. Some people are lucky, they talk to God, have a spiritual raincoat that protects them from life's storms. Many of us cling to a small group of "significant others"—those we love, those who are close friends—to affirm our identity and reflect back that self which we know to be the true self within us. For those without God and without friends, the going is hard. For those without jobs in which they can play a satisfactory role in the local community and from which they can gain the necessary sense of community the outlook is bleak. How can a young person have a satisfactory self-regarding sentiment if the society in which he or she lives says, in effect, we don't want you, don't value your skills, have no place in our set-up for you as a person? That's very sad, very bad.

Each human being is unique. Each one of us has a magic bit, a soul, a core. When you lose that, your true self, you're lost. That's why it's good to meet people who really know us. We don't have to pretend. They can see through to the centre of us, that "I" which we were, are, and will be. We grow, become multi-faceted, fly the kite of our personality high in the air, but the centre remains—we stay attached to the I. We have to steer a tenuous route between being too inner-directed and too outer-directed. We should never become detached from our essential being; we should never become so outer-directed, eager for power, wealth and possessions that we lose our own souls.

Steps towards authenticity

○ *Don't rush it.* Let other people sip at you slowly, like a good wine. This is even more essential if you're a '35 claret. Let them get the flavour, the bouquet, not gobble you up in one go.

○ *Not too many smoke canisters or false fronts.* You have to play a role (especially if you're a mother or a waitress), but be real occasionally. The rest of us want to meet you, not some cardboard cut-out you've created to protect yourself. Remember that other people are as anxious and frightened as you.

○ *Be still sometimes.* Put your feet in a bowl of warm water or go to the back door and look up at the stars for five minutes. Should your husband/partner/children make remarks about your behaviour, just tell them you're unique, a one-off with funny habits.

○ *Walk tall.* God is inside you, you're a part of the universe. Once a month go to the nearest tree and say, quietly but firmly, "I'm me." This will save you looking at your post office savings-book/driving licence/passport to find out who you are.

○ *Avoid people who pigeon-hole others.* At parties, if somebody asks you what you do, or some other question totally irrelevant to the essential you, just say "exist" (or better, "live") or say that you own a mixed sauna. (Don't use this avoidance tactic at job interviews.)

○ *Get spending and saving in perspective.* What is life for anyway, to have or to be? Play with rubber ducks, or your partner, in the bath. Life goes by very quickly. Don't say to your bath partner, "We'll be rich when we're 65." You may be, but by then you may not have the energy to push the ducks or send those little wooden boats around the lighthouse.

○ *Be daring from time to time.* Wear black underwear, say hello to that dishy man. He can't bite your head off, can he? With that kind of underwear, you need have no fear when he introduces you to his butler. Should your elastic snap as he does so, two steps to the left, a light laugh, and carry on talking as his man fetches the silver tray. While the butler's away, say to the DM, "Protect me, kind sir, from life's chill winds. This is a sign we were meant for each other." Few passionate men can resist this kind of approach.

○ *Believe that you'll grow up one day.* Also believe that you'll be Fully Mature, Lovely, Charming, Witty and 36-24-36. In the meantime, enjoy yourself. There are lots of people about who look even worse than you. On a normal distribution curve, most of us fall within the sack of turnips range. Who's counting? For every golf-ball, somewhere there's a golf-club, someone to send you bouncing (spiritually) over the fairways.

○ *Trust your feelings, your intuition.* The real self is always striving for growth, so not too many phoney selves; give your real self a chance to stand in a clear space and take in the scenery.

○ *In a hundred years time we'll all be dead.* Why anticipate events? Live for the moment!

- BUT IT WAS YOU WHO TOLD ME I SHOULD LEARN TO MAKE MY OWN FRIENDS.

Finding and keeping friends

I did a rather unwise thing a couple of months ago. I stayed overnight in Bedfordshire with an old schoolmate whom I hadn't seen for the best part of twenty years. We'd been very close friends, we'd hitch-hiked to Spain together, told all our hopes and ambitions to each other, gone around like twins. When we met, that feeling of closeness, of never having to struggle to find something to say, had gone. We were virtually strangers. What did you expect? you say. Well, yes, but I didn't think it would be as awkward as *that*. I thought we'd be able to pick up a few threads. We couldn't, not really. To tell the truth, I found it easier to talk to his family.

Before that, I had another nostalgia trip, meeting an old pal I'd known when we were both doing national service in the army. We met in London and it was disastrous. Nobody's fault. "Friend: one joined to another in intimacy and in mutual benevolence independently of sexual or family love," *OED.* The MB was there; sadly, the magic, the intimacy and the fun had vanished. I have, you'll be glad to learn, given up these little journeys in search of the happy moments of the past. These meetings can be extremely sad, embarrassing, poignant. On the whole, it's better to live where you are. Before I saw them again, both of those friends were, in my mind, still aged nineteen.

This isn't to say that I don't have old friends; I do (though not many). Cedric is an old friend. What first drew my attention to C was a curious habit of his. When the mothers used to come out on to the pavement to call in their offspring, all of us obeyed the respective call of mum fairly sharpish. There were no wasp-waisted women in our street. Some of those mothers would have frightened hell out of the US cavalry. They roamed the streets like great dinosaurs treading the primeval swamp, uttering fierce cries—some even carrying brooms. To hear was to obey. But not for Cedric.

"Ce-e-dr-eek," his mother would yell, like a witch with toothache. "Coming, dear mother," *I'd* have said. Not C. He'd stand about ten yards from her and charge straight for her pinny, ignoring the poker. "I'm *not* coming in," he'd shout as he engaged the enemy. Goodness me! I'd sooner have charged into the jaws of hell. Cedric never went in without a struggle. At school, too, he'd take on the gigantic boys. "Fight," the chant would go up, and a large circle would form. There would be Cedric, head down, fists flailing, running towards some huge lad.

After one of these sporting occasions, Cedric having incurred a torn coat and a bloodied nose, I told him, "You can be my friend." He still is. Maybe it's because in the old days I protected him; my eldest brother was the best fighter in the school.

These days, I have four male friends: Cedric, Geoff (the Wise One), Gavin, and Jon. Cedric's the only one I've known all my life; Geoff and Gavin I met as an adult; Jon I knew when he was sixteen, coming to me for advice about something or other—he kept in touch and we're now close friends. I have six women friends, none of whom I knew as a child but each of whom is now an important part of my being.

Ten friends. Is that a lot? I don't know. Friendship is about quality, not quantity. I think you're OK if you have *one* good friend: someone you can trust, call on for help, do things with, pour your heart out to, tell it how it is, for you. With a friend, you needn't apologise or feel self-conscious; you can be spontaneous, confess all, without being rejected, rebuffed, made to look a fool. It's really important to have somebody, somewhere, who accepts you as you are and doesn't rate you on some sexual or social scale to see if you pass the test. With friends, you can relax. That's vital.

Gavin came over from Winchester last week. We didn't do much. Had a couple of halves in a pub, strolled along the beach at Bournemouth. Most of the time we talked. Men tend to *do* things together: play squash, go fishing, watch the football match. I must be a bit peculiar. I like to *talk*. Gavin told me about his hopes to become a television director. (The two of us once made a television programme on young people; I presented it, he produced it. One shot shows me coming out of some bushes in Bournemouth Gardens to stand on a little bridge and do my face to camera—to this day it's known as "The Phantom Flasher" bit. Being on television isn't as easy as it looks.) I told him of my hopes to become a really good writer. If you ask me what we did all afternoon all I can say is, "Just talked." It was great.

Jon came to see me last night. Problems of the heart, again. Jon's emotional life is reminiscent of World War II. I listened, he talked. I didn't mind. I know that if I fell in love with one of the school dinner ladies, a Swiss nannygoat, or my wife's left shoe—anything—I could tell Jon about it and he wouldn't say, "You idiot." He'd listen. The only thing is that, compared with the emotional scrapes Jon gets himself into, anything I do seems very small beer. I'm looking for a three-foot Tibetan with a wooden leg (must be female) to really impress him. Compared with Jon I lead a *terribly* dull life. Listening to him makes me feel normal: that's what friends do.

Those of you with O-level maths will have noticed that I have more women friends than men. I make no apologies for this. Women, at least the ones I know, talk more, are more interested in human relationships, affairs of the heart. I'm not interested, as so many men are, in competition, who's best, showing off—seeing who can pee highest up the infant playground wall. I'm interested in *people*, especially if I needn't be afraid of making a fool of myself with them. Life's festooned with banana skins and it's pleasant, when you slip and land on your backside, to lie there and talk about it to someone who isn't scoring points for content and presentation.

But, you ask, you can't really have a true friendship with a man if you're a woman, can you? Sex always gets in the way, doesn't it? My answers are yes, you can and no, it doesn't, you can choose. Many men are obsessed by the phallus bit, riddled with anxiety that you won't see them as the Omar Sharif of Piddletrenthide. Some men would rather have a quick grapple than a relationship; for them, the world starts and ends in a bang and a whimper. The problem with these men—given that sex lasts, if you're lucky, an hour—is what will you do the rest of the time? Most of us want affection, companionship, fun. They are just as vital as the physicals. You may have to teach your man that. It can be very rewarding when he gets the idea that the two of you can actually be friends.

I like—and love—more than one woman. There are many varieties in the Rose Garden of the Affections. Take Beth. I've known her for ten years. Crimped hair, big brown eyes, Oxfam sweater and jeans, big bottom—the Old English Sheep Dog look. She's very affectionate. When Beth embraces me it's like being rolled on by a sheep; I feel all cosy, protected, warm. When I'm looking for women friends, I'm not looking for females in the model-girl class; I'm just looking for somebody I enjoy being with.

I'm not saying I don't fancy Beth. I do. But I wouldn't sleep with her. It—the sex thing—might spoil a relationship that's precious to me and I don't intend to take the risk, and neither does Beth. We're writing the script together. We decide. I *know* that a sexual relationship would disturb the magnetism that runs between Beth and myself. I know her, that girl. I've seen her nude (when the families were camping together and we sneaked off to skinny-dip in the sea); I've seen her pregnant, seen her with earache. I know she has heavy periods, gets headaches when the kids play her up, looks awful first thing in the morning. It doesn't matter. It makes it better. She is a human being, and my friend. The little sexual *frisson* that's there, underneath the relationship, is a bonus.

Yes, yes, you say, but what happens if I meet a man as a friend and then fall in love with him? Well, that's up to you. Make it clear to him (after you've figured it out yourself) what it is you want, lover or friend. If you're mad for love, nothing I say—like take plenty of cold showers and buy some worry beads—will make much difference. If you want a *friend,* tell him so. Take him to a park bench or bus shelter. Sit him down. Sit fairly near him. Tell him that there is great confusion in this world, much sorrow, so many cramped and narrow lives that you would like to restore the balance a little. Life, you could say, is a precious gift. By sharing, we share each other's magic and each other's pain; by being friendly, we teach others that they may have validity and courage, and hope.

You could quote poet and visonary Rainer Maria Rilke: *One day there will be the girl, and the woman, whose character will no longer provide a mere contrast for masculinity, but something self-justifying, something in connection with which one thinks not of a complement and a limitation, but of life and existence: the womanly person . . . This will* [much against the wishes of men, outstripped to begin with] *provide a basis for a new kind of love. The love which consists in this, that two solitudes protect and limit and greet each other.* If your man is still awake, give him a hug and say, "My pal, old buddy." Don't expect him to grasp your message all at once. There'll be other park benches, other bus stops, other times.

It's curious that many of today's young people understand the notion of companionship far better than their elders. They (the youngsters) go off in groups—camping, cycling, youth-hostelling, just having a day out together—not to have sex but to have fun and companionship. Why is it that we pathetic adults can't do the same? Beth and I go for walks through the fields; it's a feeling of freedom we're looking for and that crucial mutual affirmation of identity. Friendships are kaleidoscopic, ever-changing; sex is monochromatic, often flat, out of focus. When you're painting the picture of your life, why not use *all* the colours, or as many as you can?

Anima-animus: a balance. In both men and women. Too much animus and women become like the worst kind of men: macho, insular, aggressive distortions of a whole human being. And men, by being more sensitive and aware, less rigid, don't become weak; they become strong, worthwhile partners, well-rounded, adaptive, and life-affirming individuals. Who wants those tailor-dummy, tough, inarticulate men? They're great for shop windows, but boring to live with. It will be a great step forward when men and women learn to *like* each other, when they can say "We're just good friends" without sniggering innuendo, when male and female can be pals. Why can't I, a man, say to you, a woman, "Come hold my hand and be my friend, I like you"?

Gwen came over a few weekends ago. She's six feet tall, and every inch is quality. We went to this party on a new housing estate. Found the road, saw a light, entered the open door, starting singing in the hall. Gwen dashed into the living room. "Let's have an orgy!" she yelled. (She's awfully keen on grapes.) In a corner of the deserted room was a man, doing the ironing. It was the wrong house. The man seemed surprised, but excited; I whisked Gwen away before he could throw his shirts to the four winds and dash into the kitchen for a *chaise-très-longue* and a grape-peeler. With Gwen, the fun seems to start as soon as you go out of the door. Even if somebody gave me climbing boots for Christmas—and if she'd let me—I wouldn't sleep with Gwen. I enjoy her company *very* much. I'm not so masochistic as to throw that kind of thing away.

Honestly, I really would rather sail on the deep ocean of friendship than fiddle about collecting driftwood on an oil-stained shore. We've got to start getting this right. We can't go on with men and women as strangers, one half of the planet not knowing the other half. You could do your bit on this. Put on your little black dress, or Norwegian sweater, and get out there and see how the other half lives. If he doesn't act friendly, teach him.

Stop, you say. Here you are frollicking about through field and sand, in pub and bus stop. I don't think you quite realise my situation. (This is you, still.) I'm marooned here, in this road, with two small children. I haven't seen an interesting man in three weeks. All I seem to do is wash the kids, feed them and my husband, do the dishes, tidy the house, worry about my figure and the spot on my right cheek. We live in different worlds, you and I, buster. Friends. Freedom. Huh.

Strong stuff. (This is me.) You're quite right. If you work in an office or factory or other places which employ men, obviously you have a better chance of making friends with the opposite sex than women who are stuck at home. So let's look at the Woman At Home situation and have a bit of practical advice on that. Even if you're a Woman In Office, or a man, it will do you no harm to read the following pointers for survival.

Positive action for survival

Do think of yourself, in the far distant years to come, as a sexy old woman. Have a regular 6,000-mile service and a tune-up—have your hair done (*again?* you ask). Appearance is important to making friends and to our own self-regarding sentiment. Being married doesn't—or shouldn't—mean Go to Gaol for fifty years. Is there life after the confetti? There is.

Do get out of the house. You are unlikely to meet fascinating men in your laundry basket or in that cupboard where you stuff everything (if you know what I mean). No woman rummaging through the washing is at her best. I bet Cleopatra didn't spend the day hoping that Anthony wouldn't notice she'd recycled his socks.

Do look upon your children as human beings rather than pimples on the face of humanity. They don't want to be with you all the time: farm them out, get somebody to mind them, do a swap with a neighbour, join a playgroup—anything to give you a breather from them (and them a rest from you). Don't use your children as an excuse to avoid adult relationships. Those kids are only on loan (see Kahlil Gibran's *The Prophet*, in which he speaks to us of children; he puts it better than I do). We all know you're a wonderful mother, but how do you stand as a person? Get out; leave him with his can of light ale and *Match of the Day.* The joy of seeing him again as you come back from the poetry group will cancel the anxiety of being apart for a few hours.

Do be realistic about men. That spotty chap at Buying Antiques class may be quite interesting. Avoid macho men and (I know this is heart-breaking advice) males who look like Clint Eastwood. If he's devilishly handsome, the chances are (a) he knows it and (b) he hasn't an idea in his pretty little head.

Do be daring, imaginative, in the way you think of yourself. Join the local clog-dancers—you have nothing to lose but your breath—or morris dancers. Think of all those lovely morris men, in skirts and bells, tinkling away, *ravished* to meet you. Take a woodwork class, sign up for a *cordon bleu* cookery course, learn about photography. Think big. Give yourself a break. Life is short.

Do avoid talking about women's lib. Men need chips, mothering, and sex—in that order. But more and more of them are learning about affection and conversation. Don't beat them about the head with two thousand years of women's subjugation. Make allowances. See his etchings, admire his bookcase, listen to what he has to say about Chagall. Then, go home and tell your husband about two thousand years of being downtrodden.

Do share chores with your man. If you can't go to the PTA together, he goes one time, you go the next. Don't accept the part of Cinderella. Get to the ball. You won't meet other men if you don't go where they hang out—or, rather, *are*.

Do make the first move if you meet an interesting man. Ask him home for coffee and biscuits/to see *your* etchings/meet your partner. Most men, like basset hounds, are unable to resist biscuits. Buy a large tin, and *listen* to the IM while he's talking. Men love people listening to them; can't resist coming out with their latest Great Thought to an eager face. There *are* worthwhile men: spot them, be cheeky, ask them home. Your motives, remember, are impeccable. Here, I'm talking of friendship, not affairs. No cheating or you'll blow the pattern of relationships you've managed to build up. If it's *affairs* you're after, then take a degree in social administration, get your doctor to insert a fast-forward-wind button in your navel, and become a past mistress of disguises—you'll need all that, and a phenomenal memory, as well. My vote is with learning to be friends, first.

Friends should, in theory, take the place of all those aunts and uncles, grannies and granddads who used to be available in times of need or loneliness. Friends could be—should be?—substitutes for relatives, but I'm not sure it works like that. For one thing, an extended family wasn't age-segregated: children could mix with the elderly, adults with each other or with the young or the old. Now, we tend to mix with our peers, people of our own age. There are a few children who are, I hope, my friends. But, at the moment of writing, I have only one friend who is a senior citizen. A shame. I'd like more. I think we could learn a lot from each other across the generation gaps, as they did in the old days.

There's no reason why not. A friend is a person with whom you can feel relaxed, someone for whom you don't have to put on an act or wear a particular mask. A friend is someone you can talk to. For adults, this shouldn't preclude either children or the elderly. It often does. I think that's sad. Nowadays we tend to push old people together, keep them out of our way (as we do children, for that matter); just mix with people who have common interests and who are roughly of the same age group. That's another fenced-off tendency (besides the man/woman segregation) that cuts us off from a vast chunk of human experience and interchange.

While we're talking about families and friends, let me say loud and clear that I see no reason why members of the same family shouldn't be friends—despite that *OED* definition of friendship. I really can't understand why you shouldn't actually *like* your husband/wife/partner, enjoy his/her company: be mates. As you grow older, I think this friendship aspect becomes a crucial part of a long-term relationship. An old lady told me once that her husband had died and she missed him dreadfully. "We had such good fun together," she said. What a marvellous thing to say. She was married to him for fifty-three years. I know one or two couples who can't stand the sight of each other after five years. They've never been able to make friends with each other, you see.

It's the same with children. When they're toddlers, they need love. When they're older—say, teenagers—they need friendship just as much. It's very nice to be able to say that you're friends with your own children. I hope I am. I hope, when they finally flee the nest, they'll come back to see me not because they feel sorry for me, or see me as old and decrepit, but because they like to be with me, like me as a person, really like *me*. That's what I hope. I don't see why it shouldn't be like that. We'll have to wait and see. It would be very pleasant when I'm eighty, sitting out on the porch, if they came up the path and said, "Hi, old buddy." Then, at last, I'd know I'd cracked this bringing up children thing.

As you've probably gathered, I think friendship is vital. That's because I've had a lot of emotional rewards from my friends. It's also because I've seen people in the clinic who didn't have any friends at all. Many years ago, as a young psychologist, I'd have labelled these people "depressives", "neurotics", "anxiety cases". Somewhere along the line I stopped labelling. Now, I'd just say that they were very lonely people (and you can be lonely in a nuclear family, believe me) who didn't seem to have many, or any, friends, didn't have somebody to talk to. I was there *not* to diagnose them or to poke about in their unconscious minds; I was there to provide practical help, develop their social interests, find some kind of group in which they could learn about life—and about themselves.

I'm with Adler on this one. The neurotic's lifestyle lacks balance; there's too much emphasis on self, not enough on community feeling. If there's a sexual problem, it's usually because the neurotic (ie, the lonely person) uses sex to get the better of his or her partner, to gain superiority or sympathy. Sex should be joyful; that some people use it to gain power over others is a symptom of a pathological lifestyle. Illness, too, can be used to gain dominance or attention. It's very sad when a person has to become ill in order to be cherished. Many people do. We used to see some of them in the clinic. The attention of a psychologist, when you're suffering from a broken heart, or a sickness of the soul, is a very poor substitute for real friendship.

I first began to doubt Freudian theory when I was training for the job. In one place I worked, it was absolutely essential for everybody to have something wrong with them. If you were normal, and certainly if you were too bouncy, everybody was suspicious. I'm talking about the *trainees* here, not the patients. According to the gurus that ran the place, we had an internalised Good Mother and Bad Mother. The loss of the Good Mother made you feel depressed. The game was that you'd be asked, "How are you today?" You'd say, if you had any sense, "Depressed." If you said "I feel fine" it meant that you had "split off" the Bad Mother, weren't giving her the recognition she warranted. Something like that. I thought perhaps I ought to learn to cry at will, like good actors, then pass the course with distinction. Actually, I got fed up with the whole thing. What struck me about the high priests (not to mention the patients) was that they seemed very isolated, unreal people. "How can I listen to all this Freudian garbage you're spouting," I felt like saying to my teachers, "when your own loneliness is thundering in my ears?" I never did speak up. I wanted to pass the course. After you with the onion, please.

What success I've had in my clinic work is due to my ability (a) to listen and (b) to wear out shoe leather finding a suitable social group in which the client could learn a few social skills, make a few friends. What Melanie (17) did for the depressed Henry (16) at the youth club I found for him, I'll never know. It was presumably something I couldn't. Whatever it was, it beautifully supplemented my own counselling of the lad, especially as it took place elsewhere, in the evenings. Who made him better I can't say, but I doubt whether it was my skill in saying "Hm, hm" that did the trick. I think he reconstructed his world and Melanie helped with the bricks. I never asked, just put on case notes, *Healthy bloom on this lad's cheeks.*

There was a very posh girl who came to see me. She was one of the loneliest people I've ever met. (Can we forget about the word "depressed"?) I exceeded myself on her behalf. I got her to join a rambling society and the local Speedway Supporters Club. The ramblers went by the board. She took up with a lad with a motor bike (he'd bring her around to the clinic on the pillion) and a *very* noisy bunch of young people. Well, their bikes were noisy, but they were quite pleasant, although to be honest I'd rather stay at home and put the wireless on full blast and throw ash over myself than go to one of those speedway meetings. The mother of the girl was a bit dubious about it all; so was I. It all worked out fine. It was a resting place, an emotional oasis for the girl; it got rid of a lot of her frustrations and aggression. She's married now with two children. I see her occasionally. She drives a car. Disappointing, that. She looked very attractive, I thought, in her crash helmet and leathers.

It saddens me when I read about young mothers who are depressed. For depressed, read lonely. Instead of pills, give them the help they need to join a group, develop some social interests, contribute something towards the community. The medical model of illness isn't appropriate here. Pills don't cure loneliness. An emphasis on social responsibility, on concern for others, on the goal of *love thy neighbour* will do far more for us all. The neurotic, the depressed, the mentally ill are those who have taken a fall in the Competitive Stakes. We must learn to co-operate as well as to compete with each other. If we don't, many more of us will face emotional fences we simply can't jump. The daft thing is that life isn't a race; it shouldn't be competitive *all* of the time. We have to learn to help each other. Psychiatrists, psychologists, and social workers are a poor second-best to community feeling. Ask me the cure for depression, neurosis, I'll answer you simply: friendship. It is the best cure *I* know.

Let me say something about mobility, moving about the place, in some cases all over the country. Some people can cope with it; some can't. A friend's husband got a job in Birmingham; the family moved there from Dorset. My pal told me, "I hate it here. I always will. I lost so many good friends by moving." (Let me make it clear that I, personally, have nothing against Brum. I'm sure it can work out equally badly the other way round.) I sympathise with my pal. We used to live in Chester. We lived next door to a couple who were, and are, our friends. After *fifteen* years I still miss them terribly. I think about them regularly, see them rarely. It can be very hard when you move to a new place. Sometimes you have a real sense of loss.

What can you do about it? The only solution is the obvious one: build up a new circle of friends to replace the ones you have lost. This can be quite demanding. You have to get out there, work at it, find out what's going on, join things, go where interesting people are. It can be hard work. One woman I know, when her husband moved to London, refused to move with him. He stays there during the week, comes home at weekends. She prefers it; he doesn't. I think we all have to come up with our own answer to the question of promotion and more money *v* staying put. If you do move, you must build up a new network of relationships, a fresh emotional support system, make new friends. If you don't, you'll be awfully lonely. It's worth the initial effort.

Friendship offers trust, emotional security, comfort, practical help and—hopefully—fun, but it can't cater for *all* our needs. "I'm peculiar," a friend tells me, "I need isolation." Once in a while she gets into her Morris 1000 Traveller, goes off into the country and walks the lanes and fields by herself. When I feel crowded I go to Andorra, or Wales, or I lock myself into my study. You may, as I once had to, make do with the toilet, with two little fists banging at the door and a plaintive voice asking, "Are you in there?" ("No," you say in a high-pitched voice.)

I'm not saying we need friends all the time. But it's nice, when you've been alone (like my pal), to have friends to come back to; it's nice to have friends there when you need them. That's why it's hard to accept, can be sad, when they live far away. At times, we all have a horror of propinquity; at other times we need friendship, company. It's nice to know they're there. Good friends allow us space and understand when we want to be by ourselves. That, to me, shows that they really know how funny-peculiar we can be at times.

I may have given the impression, in talking of my own friends, that it's roses, roses all the way. This isn't how it is—not all the time. Bad times, as well as good, can strengthen the invisible bond between two people. My friend Amy went through a very bad patch. I suppose, not to put too fine a point on it, she went slightly bonkers: she started to ramble in her speech, get funny ideas, talk ceaselessly, wear everybody out. My own view of what was happening was that she was fighting off an inner loneliness, a feeling of great sadness that was slowly overwhelming her. Amy's marriage was breaking up; *nothing* seemed to be going right in her world at that time.

It would be nice to say that friends rallied round, listened, gave the support she needed. It wasn't quite like that. For about six months Amy was pretty unbearable. "How's it going?" you'd ask. You would be given a non-stop description of her woes, aches and pains, trials and tribulations, strange ideas. It was awful to listen to; made no sense. It was frightening, too. It's not pleasant to see somebody you like and can remember as a joyous, warm, fun-loving person, cracking up right under your nose. "God, I can't stand Amy at the moment," one of her other friends told me. You *have* to stand her. What are friends for?

I'm saying this because I, like you, have known or read about apparently happy people who have suddenly made journeys into the interior, had breakdowns or, tragically, have committed suicide. Could it have been prevented? I don't know. Sometimes it isn't possible to know what's going on in the secret heart of a person. All we can do, if we think a friend is in deep emotional trouble, is to be sensitive to his or her inner life and to organise as many support systems as we can around him or her. We can *go with* our friend to the GP, tell them about Marriage Guidance, the Samaritans or some other agency that could help out (and perhaps prevent that tragedy). Friendship, as I've said, isn't all roses: caring can be painful and take an effort from you.

With Carol, with Jenny, with Judy—my three other women friends—I'm just happy being with them. Judy (Geoff's wife) is so pretty that I could sit and look at her all day, except that she insists on talking about painting, and literature and music—that kind of thing—which is much more interesting than it sounds. Curious woman, Judy. She's perfect. For the last eight years I've tried to spot some kind of flaw in her. I can't. She looks like a top model, is a good cook, is clever, plays the piano and used to play hockey for the county. "It makes you want to spit," says my wife. I wouldn't know. I've never played hockey. With all three of these friends I can talk about anything. They'll listen, not put me down. I think I'm very lucky to know them.

The deliberate mistake in the Persian carpet of my existence (the flaw is sewn in since only Allah is perfect; Judy I'm still working on) is, of course, Cedric. He is the living witness to the inherent mystery of life. Last night I took him to a church hall where there was a Q and A session on terrible teenagers. I introduced Cedric to the vicar, our host, and, sadly, the vic mentioned something about when *he* was a boy. That set Cedric off on his "when I was a lad it were three to a shirt" routine. This stopped at the sight of Carol in the back row. Cedric, doing his imitation of a gorilla, loped off towards her. "Odd," said the vicar. Well put, vic. I didn't tell him that Cedric was my oldest friend. They say you can judge people by their friends, and where does that leave me?

Our friends sustain us as water and sun and rich soil sustain a plant. Without them we would wither away. With them we can be ourselves, and we can grow. If I were to write two songs, the second would be about love. The first would be about friendship.

One last point. It's difficult for me, as a man, to write about friendships between women, but as an outsider in this, my impression is that women can—and do—gain tremendous emotional and social support from friendships with each other. Indeed, I sometimes suspect that the roles that they have to play within the family, or in pursuing a career, or in trying to be exactly what their husbands/partners/lovers want them to be, make it essential for women these days to have close women friends—if only to relax and be themselves, for five minutes.

As the divorce rate increases, as more and more marriages break up, as the notion of a series of monogamous relationships becomes a more accepted pattern, as we try to find an answer to the emotionally stifling effects of the nuclear family and the continuing abuse (financial, vocational, physical and emotional) of women in our society, I am sure that the safety-net, the support system, of women's friendships with other women will become even more crucial. I'm not surprised that women cling to each other in friendship. When I look at some of the men around me, I can understand why women need each other so much.

Points to remember about friendship

○ *Friends are vital.* They are the *dramatis personae* with whom we play out our sexual, vocational, or family life.

○ *You have to work at friendship.* Do take time off from thinking about your family, your job, your duties, to make friends. Try to get out and meet a variety of people: this is the path to that significant other, that special person, a close friend. You'll never make a CF if you stay at the kitchen sink/in front of the television/head down in the laundry basket.

○ *Friends can be of either sex.* Women still tend to make close friends with other women, men with other men. This is altering, slowly. Make it alter more rapidly by your own efforts to cultivate men as friends. In my view, platonic (and very rewarding) relationships with the opposite sex *are* possible.

○ *Keep the family in perspective.* It's not the whole of your life; you still need friends. Don't let the family make so many demands on you that you stop looking for (or neglect existing) friendships outside the home. Your family will get more from you if you insist on keeping your own friends and make sure that you meet them regularly. Give your friends the importance they deserve.

○ *Cut across age (and sex) barriers.* The wider, more varied, your circle of friends, the more you learn about life, and yourself.

○ *Show your friends affection.* If they don't get warmth, spontaneity from you, whom *do* they get it from? We all know there's a taboo on touch, demonstrated affection, in our society. Ignore it. Cherish your friends. You like them. Show it.

○ *Women aren't chattels or ornaments to be used to cement friendships between men.* Don't rely on your spouse/partner to supply all your emotional needs. That's the royal road to spiritual isolation.

○ *Try to see your own family as friends.* The family in which people like each other, are friends, stays together. Why not?

○ *Don't retreat too far into yourself if you lose a good friend.* You *will* mourn, feel sad, have a sense of loss. But remember that there are a lot of people out there who would be glad of you as a friend.

○ *Start up a class, group, or club.* I mean anything from a mum-and-toddler group to a Keep the Footpaths Open club. Doing things together, having a common interest, a shared goal, is an effective way of sparking off spontaneous friendships. If your children see you making and keeping friends, they'll quickly latch on to the notion of human friendship, people caring about each other. It's a central lesson in life. This planet won't last too long unless it starts getting hold of the idea, so set a good example.

Pick your worry

Everybody I know is worried about *something.* My younger daughter's apprehensive about her O-levels coming up later this year. She asked me to give her some help with her French oral. "*Quelle heure est-il?*" I began. "*Il fait beau,*" she replied. The secret of these things, I've told her, is to steer the conversation your way, but I didn't mean that you should talk about China if the examiner's on about, say, Paris. "*Mon Dieu,*" said my daughter, after my next query, "*j'ai un* complete blank." She rushed into my study to look for a book called *French in Two Weeks.* "This," I said to my wife, "is the age of *Angst,* of fear, of dread." For this great insight I was told to can it. "*Nous vivons,*" I shouted to the YD, "*dans une époque d'anxiété.*" From the study came a faint voice and the words, "*Six heures.*" Some people who worry have cause to be worried. Let's have the truth around here.

It's curious what people worry about. Cedric, for example, never worries about money. He owes his bank manager several thousands of pounds and has just borrowed a couple of thou to buy a second-hand Mercedes. "Any repairs on that will cost you a bomb," I've told him. "I'll borrow some more money, then," he says. That kind of thing would worry me sick. I hate owing anybody anything, even having the relatively small mortgage on my house. My mother—besides the always-airing-underwear thing—told me that you should never get into debt. I'd worry myself sick, but Cedric positively revels in it, boasts about how much he owes and to whom. Faced with his debts, I think I'd crack up with anxiety.

What Cedric worries about is his garden. He grows vegetables: peas, runner beans, sprouts, that kind of thing. It means nothing to me. "Bloody slugs," shouts Cedric, running out with an aerosol can. Sitting in the garden with him is an appalling experience. If he sees a bird he jumps up, grabs a stick, and chases it. He has a scarecrow, aluminium foil *and* wire netting to keep them away. His garden is like Colditz. "You don't get vegetables as fresh as that in the best London restaurants," says C when you have a meal with him. I know, but is it worth the trouble of getting up in the night and prowling the garden with a torch to see if the slugs are tunnelling their way through to the cauliflowers? Is it worth shouting "*Schweinehund*" every time a sparrow lands on your apple tree? His garden is immaculate.

Our garden is chaos. Yesterday, I spotted four woodpigeons, a green woodpecker (yellowy, really, with a red cap and a bird call that sounds like my Aunt Rose laughing at a dirty joke), a robin, a squirrel, two blackbirds, a black dog, a ginger cat plus a mother and child—total strangers. They know quality, grass-wise. We've lost people in the undergrowth and had to send out search parties. God knows what's at the far end among those bushes; I've never been that far.

"A weed is no more than a flower in disguise," I've often told my wife. "Where's the book of instructions for this hoe?" I ask Cedric and recite from my deckchair, "*The kiss of the sun for pardon/The song of the birds for mirth.*" Cedric rushes off after the squirrel, hoe in hand. "*One is nearer God's Heart in a garden/Than anywhere else on earth,*" I tell him when he comes back. "Dorothy Gurney, 1858–1932," I say. I'd hate Cedric to think I was making it up. "Those sodding squirrels will chew up your oak trees," says Cedric. "Bloody pests," he says. Sometimes he can be less than poetic. The only precaution I take in the garden is not to wear flowered underpants. The man over the road keeps bees.

What does make me anxious is this house we live in. Our kitchen is like the Black Hole of Calcutta; at one time we were thinking of renting it out to Hammer Films. Anybody with a spider phobia would go stark raving mad in there. In our house we have carpets discolouring, walls crumbling, paper peeling, window frames rotting, boards creaking, roof leaking and two chimney stacks leaning. What, Old Friend? Art thou afear'd, fretful? Frankly, yes. I woke up one morning recently to find a black fungus growing on the bedroom wall. "A mushroom farm, we could all be rich!" I yelled (I was half-asleep at the time). "Spring, dwarling," said my wife. Is that an order? I sprang. "Gerroff," shouted my wife. People lose all sense of time and priority when they're dreaming.

To create tidiness in the house I've just bought this huge industrial vacuum cleaner. *Whoosh.* Sucks up spiders, cockroaches, gunge, comics, plastic bags, pins, newspapers—the lot. A pleasure to use it. "Where's my shoes?" the YD asked yesterday. "*Are* my shoes," I told her. Got to get the grammar right, what with O-levels coming up. Carol walked past our house last week, on her way to the park. "Summer, tra la," she shouted. I was standing by our front door with the IVC. "What the hell are you doing?" she asked. "Fighting the ants," I said. That same evening I spotted a bluebottle on our giant white Habitat lampshade. To the cupboard. *Whoosh.* We now need a new GWHL. It's just one more little thing that I'll have to worry about.

Some very stupid things are written about worry. I mean, we all know it's absolutely useless to say to someone, "Don't worry." It only makes things worse. When I'm due to go to the dentist, I worry. Nothing you can say will have any effect on the crux of the matter: how many fillings is it this time? When I'm in the chair, I lie back, think of sex—or soldiers having their legs sawn off at the Battle of Waterloo. I don't have an injection, all I want is for my dentist, a very good one, to get on with the job and get it over with. Nothing you or he can say will alter the fact that it *is* painful and rather undignified. "This won't hurt." So he says. "Don't think about it too much." Save all that nonsense. Pain is pain; don't tell me that what I'm feeling doesn't exist.

Let's have a few facts. If a large bull strolled into your living room, you'd feel a certain amount of fear and prepare for action. Your brain would send a message to the adrenal glands and adrenalin would pour into your bloodstream. You'd go pale as blood was diverted from the skin (and other places) to help to prime your muscles, your heartbeat would get faster, sugar would be released from the liver to give you more energy, and your whole sympathetic-adrenal system would co-ordinate all the changes taking place to help you to cope with this emergency.

In the face of danger, we have only three options: fight, flight, or imitation. Take the bull situation (last option first). You could pretend to be another bull. I don't advise this. Bulls may be colour-blind, but they're not that stupid. You could pretend to be a cow. This has obvious drawbacks, especially if the strategy is successful. You could (second option) make slowly and calmly for window or door. Last (first option, now), you could reach out for a red cushion and stand and fight. Unless you've had experience in a *corrida de toros* I can't advise this, not even if you've seen bullfights on Spanish television or done Spot the Bull in those Spanish newspaper competitions. Bulls, close up, look larger than they do on television. My advice, taking a look at you and this imaginary bull, is to put your adrenalin to good use by making for the nearest exit.

When we lived nearer to nature, it was quite easy to see the use of adrenalin and the quick decision regarding fight, flight, or imitation. Faced with a tiger or crocodile, you had to think quickly or lose your life. In the wild, there are a lot of dangerous situations, and any sensible person must keep his or her brain (and adrenal glands) at the ready. Should you relax, lose your concentration, a boa constrictor will get you if a tiger doesn't. Danger is everywhere, once you leave cave, encampment, or bamboo hut.

It's surprising how this kind of Real Danger keeps you on your toes. In Kenya, I came into a clearing once where there was a deer. His nostrils twitched and he was off like a shot; he didn't like the look or smell of me. On the same outing (cross my heart, this is true) I was going along the bank of a stream when I suddenly came face to face with an enormous rhinoceros. "Whoops," I said, and backed away. (Flight: I'm no hero.) The rhinoceros's knees crumpled and he sank to the ground with a pained look in his eyes. He'd fainted or dropped dead with surprise (or horror—I was wearing the most awful baggy shorts at the time). Nobody would believe me except my Masai scout (he was just behind me). "Rhinos don't faint," I told him. "They charge." He just cleaned his teeth with a twig and said nothing. He wasn't interested in theories.

Away now from the forest and back to the concrete jungle. Are there any real dangers lurking in Gasworks Terrace or Acacia Avenue? Are there enemies and Wild Things which, if we do nothing about them, will make us feel anxious and afraid? My guess is that there are, but most of the dangers don't have stripes, spots or horns. Nevertheless, the dangers we face are real enough—or at least the *feeling* that we are in danger is real enough—so there's little consolation in pointing out to somebody who lives in Wapping or Milton Keynes that things would be more fraught in the African jungle. "You haven't seen my telephone bill," somebody says pragmatically. "Don't talk to me about rhinos. I'm talking about *real* stress." I'm willing to believe this. In the jungle, whatever else you may get, you don't get those brown envelopes coming through the letter box, the fear that if the gas or electricity bill doesn't finish you off then HM Inspector of Taxes will.

Carol is the most terrible worrier. I was telling her once how in Africa I would lie in the forest and hear a symphony of animal noises: monkeys jabbering, crickets squeaking, wart-hogs grunting, snakes slithering, big cats growling, frogs croaking. Nature was tuning up under the stars as the large and small made for the water-hole or just commented on the action. "Beautiful, Carol," I said. "Like Beethoven's Fifth." She told me that she knew what I meant.

Sometimes, said Carol, she'd lie in bed, Arthur snoring beside her, and think of all her worries. Money. The house. The size of her feet. Bills. Her weight. Whether to go out with Paul again, just to a beach party. What do people wear at beach parties? Her face. Arthur getting the sack. Her bottom (too big). Her breasts (too big). Her ears (too big). The tree in the garden falling on the house, smashing in the roof, making them homeless. The photos that she'd taken in and never collected. The three library books that were overdue. "It was like your experience, T," she said. "A symphony. A symphony of worry. I'm going to list my worries and let a massed choir sing them, like Verdi's *Requiem*."

I told Carol that Guiseppe Verdi's name in English would be Joe Green. "*La Traviata*, by Joe Green," said Carol. (She's into singing and amateur operatics. Carol reckons you meet a nice class of man at this sort of thing, especially the tenors.) I've told Carol that she could make a list of her worries, but this doesn't work for everybody. Some people end up worrying about how long the list is. Carol, I'm afraid, is a chronic worrier. She feels that something dreadful is about to happen—even though it never has. She has got into the habit of worrying about everything.

This rather nasty state of mind is quite irrational. I mean, there are enough real dangers in life, especially if you have children, without making them up as you go along, imagining some terrible catastrophe, some embarrassing situation that *might* occur. It's no good saying to Carol, "Cheer up, it may never happen." With her, that's besides the point. She suffers from what's known in the trade as *free-floating anxiety*. Every situation is loaded with possible danger. It's nothing specific, just a feeling that there's danger about, the Fates are just about to line you up for a sharp karate chop to the back of the neck. Anxiety is fear spread out thin. C's anxiety seems to have spread out over and oozed into every action that she takes or even contemplates. With worriers like Carol, you can't urge them to be cheerful or tell them that worse things happen at sea. They don't have to sail in boat in a force 10 wind to experience fear; they can experience it in their own homes, in front of a warm fire. It's not very pleasant to live like that. Last summer I remember saying to Carol that it was a beautiful day. "Is it?" she asked me, looking around in a distracted kind of way, as though she expected Indians to ride into her back garden and pierce her with arrows. "There are no Red Indians in Dorset," I've told her. "How the hell do you know who lives in Dorset?" snaps Carol.

I know quite a few people who are, like Carol, always anxious, who experience acute attacks of anxiety which don't seem to be related to anything in particular. I once had a young student who worried about *everything*. He came in to see me one morning. "I can't understand it," he said. "Everything's going well. My love life, the flat, the work. I'm really worried about it all. There must be something I've forgotten." He sat in front of me, wringing his hands, a first-division, natural-born worrier. "Have you finished that essay I gave you to do?" I asked him. "Oh, God!" he yelled. "I knew it!" He shook my hand and went out happy. He needed to worry about something and I, generous soul, had given him a clothes peg upon which to hang his nameless dreads, something specific to be anxious about and concentrate on.

What strikes me about anxiety is the sheer prevalence of it. Some years ago I gave a behaviour questionnaire to some twelve hundred school children (or, to be more accurate, I asked the teachers concerned to fill in the questionnaires for every member of the class). One section of the form concerned anxiety. I was astonished to find how many normal, ordinary (ie, able to cope) children were anxious. In one class, *every* child scored highly for anxiety. When I went to see the teacher to check up on this odd result, I noted that she fidgeted, tugged at her ear, moved restlessly around the room, couldn't sit still and never stopped talking. Perhaps the children got it from her. That still didn't explain all the other anxious children in other schools.

The curious thing was that these normal children were *more* anxious than a group of disturbed children who were attending the child guidance clinic and who'd also been the subject of this questionnaire. I went to a colleague and asked him about the enigmatic result. "What does it mean?" I queried. He thought for a good five minutes. "It means," he said, "that if you're not anxious these days, you must be slightly barmy." That's not quite the way I'd express it, but I knew what he meant. With adults, too, from my observation, if you're not worried about something nowadays, you are a deviant from the norm, the odd one out.

Anxiety is the price we pay for being civilised, for bottling up our emotions, deferring the gratification of all our needs and impulses. Worry is the bill that all of us have to pay for conforming to social norms, other people's expectations of us. Human beings need to conform, to belong, to have status in the group. Often, it's fear of being rejected by the group that makes the individual strive far beyond the point where there is any personal satisfaction from all the endeavour. It's fear of loneliness that motivates many of us; we all want to belong, to be cherished, to be loved. If we don't receive enough love (and who does?), we strive even harder for possessions, for status, for social prestige, for money.

If you ask people what it is that they want, they'll probably say, "To be happy." The sad thing is that wealth, knowledge, possessions and a higher standard of living don't bring happiness. Many of the things for which we strive are a substitute for love. We find that hard to admit to ourselves, but our feelings tell us the truth. The truth is that often we are travelling along the road to nowhere. No wonder many of us worry. We have cause to be worried; there's nothing more worrying than to examine your life and find it meaningless.

An acquaintance of mine has a thriving business, a large house and a duodenal ulcer. What he needs, he's told me (as he buzzes about like a blue-arsed fly), is surgery to get rid of his ulcer. *What you need*, I could tell him, *is to realise that life is very precious and yours may well come to an abrupt end if you go on like this*. The ironic thing is that he could afford to go to the south of France three times a year if he chose. He doesn't take *any* holiday. "I'm too busy," he says. It's crazy. Instead he'll go to his GP and sit there, hoping for surgery. Friend, you're travelling fast, but where are you going?

When I said that the price of conformity in our fast-moving, competitive society is high, I meant it. Take psychosomatic disorders. I estimate, on the basis of past surveys, that roughly half of those people who go to see their family doctors are suffering from emotional problems. The patient will tell the doctor that he/she is suffering from headache/flu/ulcers/backache/arthritis/lethargy. The doctor, who knows that emotional states can be reflected in physical symptoms, may simply not have the time to find out what's really wrong with the patient, or may know but feel powerless to anything about it. To do something effective about it, the doctor would have to prescribe a change of attitude, a less stressful way of life, and a different value system. What doctor has the courage to tell such a patient the truth? Anxiety, dis-ease, is the cost of telling lies to ourselves and being willing to have them confirmed by others.

Some people wish to be told that they qualify as "ill". It is a label, an identity card, that only the doctor can give them. As they come out of the surgery, these patients can say, "I am sick; therefore, I am. And I have the prescription to prove it." How tragic that to be recognised as being ill is better than being ignored, being no one at all. Better to say "I have a duodenal ulcer" than to say "I haven't got the vaguest notion of who I am or what life is supposed to be about." Give me the pills, doctor, for I seek the road to happiness but know not where to go, nor who I'm supposed to be.

The body's general preparedness to fight off illness is crucial and this, in my view, can be affected by anxiety and emotional factors. With patients suffering from heart attacks, it has been observed that when a nurse holds the patient's hand, the heartbeat can become more normal, more regular. Give *me* enough affection and I'll take my chances on becoming ill.

Stress can lower the body's resistance to disease. Stress can also kill. What surprises me is not that stress kills so many people but that it doesn't kill more. I know a man who drives his car every working day through heavy traffic. In the office, he's faced with daily decision-making, constant stress, worry. At weekends he works in the garden and is always doing jobs around the house. He hardly ever stops; he never seems to rest, to be at peace with himself. "My doctor," he's told me, "says I've got high blood pressure and that I've got to take it easy. How the hell can I take it easy? We've got that order to get out next week." He eats a big breakfast, has lunch every day, eats an enormous evening meal. He's now two stone overweight. He smokes forty cigarettes a day, never walks anywhere if he can use the car.

"When I'm sixty," he tells me proudly, "I'll have a pension *and* own this house." He waves his arm, points to the impressive wall-to-wall carpets. The truth is you're lucky to be alive now, old pal, let alone in fifteen years' time. You're a living witness to the fact that some bodies can be abused for years without giving up the fight. I wouldn't bet on you reaching sixty, though. Don't hold your breath on collecting your pension: you have so much stress in your life that by my calculations you ought to be dead now.

By stress I don't mean hard work. I know a lot of people who have worked hard all their lives and look set to live to a ripe old age. Hard work does nobody any harm, and regular physical exercise can do a body good. Stress is a subjective state—a feeling of not being able to cope, being in a situation where you can't succeed, having to take decisions too quickly, being under unremitting pressure.

Stress can kill you, anxiety can impair your functioning level, and worrying about a problem doesn't help to solve it—so what should we do about worry? I think we should divide worries into two groups: (a) worries we can do nothing about and (b) worries we *can* do something about. Mostly, you'll find, worries fall into the second category. If something's worth worrying about, it's worth open discussion, even *doing* something about. The best thing to do with anxieties, that fear spread thin around your heart, is to get them out into the open and hold them up to the light where we can all get a good look at them.

Take Arthur, Carol's husband. He often says to me, "I worry about the big issues: the size of China's army, Russia's naval superiority, the Third World, whether West Ham will win the FA Cup. I let Carol worry about food, money, furniture—trivial things like that." Arthur's cheating, I'm afraid. He couldn't care less about the Third World. He is worried about the darts team, and there he *is* effective. He'll go to all sorts of trouble to pick a good team, try to get players from other pubs to join his squad. A very effective worrier, Arthur, letting Carol look after day-to-day living. I'd be very worried—as Carol is—if I were a woman married to that kind of man.

Among Carol's myriad other worries are three specific ones that might be worth looking at. "Every month," Carol tells me, "I'm worried that I might be pregnant." Fair enough. Most sexually active woman share that worry, except for the few who worry that they're *not* pregnant. "I'm also worried about the nuclear situation," says Carol. So am I, flower. "The third thing I'm worried about is the state of my eyes; I'm really getting short-sighted. The other day a policeman stopped me in the car and I thought it was a Salvation Army officer trying to sell me a copy of the *War Cry.* I offered him 10p before I noticed that he had the wrong hat on." Join the club, C. There are a lot of short-sighted people about. I, personally, have been in ladies' loos all over the country.

First, pregnancy. All Carol can do about that is either to persuade Arthur and her lovers to have vasectomies or else to take the best advice available and choose the right contraceptive for her, and go for regular check-ups. In fact, she does this, but it still doesn't stop her worrying about it. With the nuclear issue, Carol can read up on the facts, get to know the arguments. If she feels that strongly about it, she could join CND, write to the local and national papers, go on marches, stand up and be counted in the debate. It's either that or taking Arthur's view: "When we go, we'll all go together." Carol does go to meetings about nuclear issues, but I think they make her worry even more. For the short-sightedness, Carol really should go to a good optician. In this, she's being naughty. She hasn't done anything about it so far.

You can't be strictly logical—a female version of Mr Spock—about worries, but you *can* talk to other people about them. I worry when my two oldest children borrow the car. Will they get back safely? Will anything terrible happen to them? The only thing you can do in this kind of situation is to mention it to other people with teenagers who drive (they worry, too, which is some kind of consolation), and to remember that you can't keep your eye on young people twenty-four hours a day. You have to trust them to be sensible. My daughter lived in Paris for a year; my son is in America. Sure, I worried, and I still worry, but they have to learn to look after themselves, to be responsible. Worry is the price we pay for not keeping them locked up, ineffective, tied to our apron strings. It's reassuring, though, to realise that you share this kind of worry with quite a few other parents.

Back to Carol. I think she makes three major mistakes. First, Carol is too immersed in her own problems. There are, unknown to her or ignored by her, people out there with what I call Real Problems. There are people who can't walk or talk or see or hear; people who have to lie in bed, every day of their lives; people who can only move their heads; people paralysed from the waist down; people who live every day with a physically and/or mentally handicapped child. There are people who have suffered in road accidents; people who suffer from incurable illnesses; people who have suffered terrible bereavement.

The disabled people that I've met have been very courageous. I suppose if you meet lots of other people who are courageous, you learn to be brave. Or perhaps being disabled just means that you get life's more trivial problems, the kind of things that you and I worry about, into a more realistic perspective. I see nothing but courage in a blind person learning to cope, a person in a wheel chair being determined to live as normal a life as possible, or a child smiling in the face of the most appalling physical disability.

Consider how miserable many able-bodied people are. Most of us don't know how lucky we are. I think we can learn a lot from the disabled. A bit more contact with those who have massive handicaps would help us to put our "problems" into a more appropriate framework—and we might even stop worrying about ourselves and start thinking about what we could do to help someone else.

Carol has also got into the *habit* of worrying. She doesn't live today; she's always worrying about tomorrow. Dale Carnegie advises his readers to live in "day-tight compartments". I agree with that. It's what's at hand that counts. "What shall I wear for the party this weekend?" asks Carol. As she asks me, the sun is shining, it's a beautiful day. Who cares about the weekend? Let it look after itself. "Take a quick decision on Saturday, Carol," I tell her. Don't waste time worrying about those things which you can do nothing about at the moment. By the time the event arrives you'll be so exhausted thinking about it that you'll probably make a worse mess of it than if you hadn't bothered about it one iota. Do what you can now. Today is the first day of the rest of your life. Tomorrow may be painful, but even if it is, it's nothing like the pain you experience from spending today worrying about tomorrow.

The third mistake Carol makes is that she's the most incredible perfectionist. Everything has to be just so. She dreads making a mess of something and lives in constant fear of failure. Carol thinks that life is the Hunt for Perfection—in clothes, love affairs, food, looks, ankles, bottoms. I'm fairly sceptical about all this; I doubt whether there's much perfection this side of the grave. As Plato said, somewhere there's a perfect chair. I've never seen it. If you don't mind, I'll sit on this one right here.

I don't think we can achieve perfection, or win all the time. I was immensely cheered to read Stephen Pile's *The Book of Heroic Failures.* It made me feel better about the dinner I went to in a brown suit, where everybody else was in evening dress. Thank God I didn't wear jeans. Actually, it didn't matter one little bit. My talk went down all right, and I doubt whether anybody thought anything other than that I was slightly eccentric, or too poor to own a dinner jacket, or mad about brown. Since I looked out of it, I was determined to enjoy myself and enter into the spirit of the thing. We all had a ball and nobody was scoring me for sartorial elegance—not in *that* suit. So many of the things we think matter desperately don't matter at all.

With Carol, her perfectionism sometimes takes the form of Making Exactly The Right Impression. Carol puts on make-up and changes her dress when she goes to see the Lovely Lady who lives over the road. "Why?" I've asked her. "Go as you are. If she's as perfect as you say, then the more natural you are, the better. Let her compete with somebody else." People sometimes like us *for,* as well as despite, our faults. The reason I like Mr Spock is because of his pointed ears. If he had perfect, shell-like ears (like me), I wouldn't be able to take his comments. Why strive after perfection when you can have life and friendship?

I'm not exaggerating when I say I'm surrounded by anxious people. Some men and women I know are like balloons you blow up in the morning and—*pssst*—they're off, flying about the place with no sense of direction at all. Others are like those toy airplanes you wind up with an elastic band. Up in the air they go, zoom, straight as a die, only to come down again a few seconds later with a dull thud. What's it all about?

Worry is a waste of time. It can become a daily propitiation ceremony that we go through to assuage the gods. I imagine if there are any gods sitting up there on the cumulus-nimbus, they'll be judging you on your actions rather than your worries—or excuses. Life's *always* been hard, down through the ages. It's not life that's the enemy, it's the way you look at it. Don't send me a postcard from Monte Carlo saying, *Am enjoying the sun and the nude bathing, but it's only Tuesday.* Tackle Wednesday when it comes, is my advice.

Tips to see the inveterate worrier through the day

○ *Realise that the pain of worry is often worse than the event you dread.* As Seneca put it, "We are often more frightened than hurt, our troubles spring more often from fancy than from reality."

○ *Accept a certain amount of anxiety.* Without any anxiety, we'd never get anything done.

○ *Don't think too much—get on with it!* Do your best. Perfection is to do with God, or possibly that lady over the road. Do the very best you can, then to hell with it.

○ *Don't dread the rustling of the grass or look for trouble behind every door.* Grief and pain have limits; fear and apprehension have none. Have courage, dare to *do*. It can't be any worse than sitting there, worrying about it.

○ *Discuss your worries with friends and bring your hidden fears out into the open.* It's surprising, and comforting, to find that other people have nameless dreads, little or big anxieties—just like you do.

○ *If you're tense, attend an evening relaxation course.* Learn to hang loose with yoga or music and movement—or strenuous exercise! Say STOP IT to worry. Rushing about is a habit that gets you nowhere fast, so *use* that energy.

○ *Take time to sit down with your feet up.* When I was at school somebody spread the message that the world was going to end at three o'clock that afternoon. It didn't. If the world comes to an end while you're lolling in the armchair, peeling yourself a grape, at least you'll be comfortable. My guess is that the world will continue to spin on its axis even when you and I aren't supervising it.

○ *If you have a problem, get the best possible advice you can.* The advice may be from a doctor/friend/lawyer/other expert. Don't try to figure everything out by yourself. You need to talk it out. What are those experts, or friends, for? A problem shared, looked at from a number of different angles, may not seem so insuperable after all. Don't sit on a problem for weeks; you are not a broody hen. Remember: discussion prevents despondency.

○ *Play it cool sometimes.* Go to the cinema the evening before that vital interview; don't sit for hours with your hat on before meeting your new man. If you get all tensed up, you'll never do yourself justice. Relax, and let the real you shine through.

○ *Take an interest in others and have a bit of sympathy for them.* If you think about yourself all the time, I'm not surprised you're worried. Don't keep looking in the mirror; it's *other* people who have to look at your face. Let them worry about it, while you're enjoying life and perhaps doing something for others. If you can manage to help somebody else along the way, I doubt whether he or she will even notice that pimple on your forehead, or the generous size of your bottom. It's you who's counting, not them. Certainly not me.

The search for love

Love has many faces. It can be companionable, cruel, irrational, heady, poignant, joyous, tragic. 'Tis love that makes the world go round. It's my great passion and, to tell you the truth, my only reason for living.

I learned about love from the outside at the child guidance clinic, working as an educational psychologist, where many of the children I saw needed only a daily dose of affection. They used to snuggle up against me at my desk, these emotionally deprived children, and I'd put my arm around them and talk to the mothers, try to show them that love is essential to us all. I began to wish with some of the mothers I saw—who found it hard to love because they themselves hadn't been loved as children—that we could bottle love, dish it out in huge spoonfuls, give it as medicine. But love isn't like that, it has to come from people, not served up in handy bottles.

Life, in principle, is very simple. It is a battle between *Eros* and *Thanatos:* love *v* death. Children know that; they see the world more clearly than we do. "The greatest terror a child can have," says John Steinbeck in *East of Eden,* "is that he is not loved, and rejection is the hell he fears." We all fear rejection, want love but are afraid of love. I never wondered why I saw children in that clinic who had resorted to theft, arson, violence, and vandalism in order to gain some attention. Why shouldn't they? People *can* die without love.

It is strange who, or what, people love, I think many people have second-choice loves: their first loves have been barred from them, so they have to love someone or something else. They still love, though. Everybody does, even if it's only money, or themselves, a place or a memory.

There was this girl, fifteen years old, tall with it, beautiful in a white dress, who came to see me in the clinic one sunny afternoon. I noticed her cornflower-blue eyes, tanned skin, and shapely legs. I found that she was warm, charming, intelligent. Tess was a person whom it would be easy for someone to love. She looked, and acted, about eighteen and was always trying to get me to go to the pub in the evening and have a drink with her. I explained that wasn't in the rules; I didn't meet clients socially. On the way home I'd buy myself another St Christopher medal to ward off my unprofessional thoughts as I sped along the road.

She was rather a naughty young lady, if moral judgements are your bag. She freely volunteered the details of her sex life and I, prurient soul, listened with interest, although I didn't much like it when she probed into mine. "Have you ever done it in the back of a lorry?" she asked me. "Or on the kitchen table?" I replied that I'd never be able to get up on either (a Freudian slip). Anyway, she ran away from home a lot (mostly on long-distancers) and it was thought that she might be in need of care and protection. The note didn't specify from what.

We talked about love. I told her about Thomas Hardy who loved only himself. Hardy *could* love, but only if the person were dead, or elsewhere. Why that should be, I'm not sure. When Hardy died they interred his ashes in Westminster Abbey, while his heart was placed in the grave of his first wife in the little country churchyard at Stinsford. "In life," I added, ever the philosopher, "it's a good thing to keep your heart and your body in the same place, if you can."

We turned to a love for places. The girl told me that she loved Liverpool: she'd been there in a cement lorry (in the front). Hail, Caesar, Ruler of the World and certain parts of the Dingle, it's curious how many people love Liverpool.

I've been to Liverpool, and seen old men measuring out their lives in half-pints in the pubs; I've been to New Brighton, over the water, seen a three-legged cat in the deserted Victoria Road, heard the numbers being called to the old and the lonely in open-fronted bingo halls, seen the wet newspapers blowing down the street, the wood-filled windows of Birkenhead North and the second-hand shops in Wallasey, one-time prosperous dormitory town of Liverpool whose citizens would walk around the top deck of the *Royal Daffodil*, carrying umbrellas, on their way to the big city. There are parts of Merseyside, once prosperous and attractive, which have died through want of love. Places have a spirit—loved or unloved—just like people.

I went to call on Tess's parents. They weren't Monty-Python, bursting-through-walls awful; I suppose that they were both—as individuals—fairly reasonable, but they didn't seem to have anything in common or to like each other very much. The mother told me that she'd been saved by God, and I was going to ask her to put in a word for Birkenhead North, but I didn't. Mum had an infant, a girl of three, a little afterthought born when Tess was twelve. Tess was a shut-out child. Mother was saved, and the baby; she loved neither Tess nor her husband. The first was "lustful" and the second was "slothful"—both deadly sins. She told me so. That's an interesting way of looking at things, but not very loving.

Father was more friendly, but hopeless. He showed me his stamp albums. Stamps? I couldn't get anything out of him except that Tess was heading for mischief. "She's deep, that one," he'd say, showing me his first-day issues. Deep? "She's heading for trouble," he'd say, pointing out his pride and joy, a penny black. *She's in trouble already, buster*, I felt like telling him, but it was no use. He had no affection for her either. Some people are born in circumstances which resemble being saddled in the enclosure at Epsom when the race is on at Newbury. "Love her, you fucking bastards!" I felt like shouting at them both. I didn't. There is no way you can make people love somebody, or something, if they don't.

Some of us (like me) think that without love you might as well be dead. A little strong? Well, can we agree that love is a pretty marvellous thing, and it's just getting your share of it that seems to be the snag? Lots of my friends are crazy about love, want it badly, are convinced of its importance. It's locating it, finding the right person, at the right time, in the right place, that seems to lead to difficulty.

That is why so many of us are keen on romantic novels. You know the sort of thing: all about LOVE. He's called Quentin, she Imogen. (Sad that in real life he's Arthur, you're Doreen.) They meet at Heathrow, he's been on a dig at Rhodes for the last three years (that should make him sex-starved, if anything could), his family owns a farm in Devon. Your eyes meet over the luggage carousel (you're in this). You feel a pounding in your heart. Waiting for a taxi, *he*'s there, right in front of you in the queue. No mistaking that tall, spare frame, scar on right cheeck, large brown hands, searching Aegean-sea eyes. This is a man who peels off top layers, gets at what's underneath. You step forward together, for the same taxi.

"Fulham?" he asks you. "I'm Imogen," you say, teeth sparkling in the sunshine, a *frisson* running through the tiny blonde hairs that cover your sunburned arms. "Why don't we share?" Lovely. As you jump into the taxi, he's thinking that you're the most beautiful person he's ever seen in his life and he's already fallen in love with you. As the taxi sets off towards London, there in the back seat your fingers have entwined. He tells you of his widowed mother, aged sixty-eight, who can no longer manage the farm by herself.

You know that if you hang in there long enough, you're eventually going to get to the row of dots or the bedroom. With romantic novels, all you need to bake the cake of love is two people (usually a man and a woman), a bit of confusion, a question (will they make out together or will a Malevolent Fate/his mother put the boot in?), a story line (difficulties—they resolve them, or don't), an ending. I like happy endings myself. I can't stand it when a shot rings out, or she walks through the door of Marks & Spencer into the rain. Please make it end happily, like it should—but often doesn't in real life.

In real life, I'm Tom, you're Beryl. We never go to Heathrow but, if we do, we take a bus not a taxi. In the queue, I'm going to Weymouth, you're going to Wapping. Even if we got into a taxi together, actually going to the same place, I'd say the wrong thing sooner or later or you'd mention that you adore cities, can't stand the country, don't like J D Salinger, love marzipan and cold tripe (not necessarily together), and don't like men who try to look younger than they are. I'd know, then, that you were not the soul mate, the other half of the cracked cup, for whom I'd been searching. I'd never get to see what's underneath; you'd never get to meet my mother. It's the difference between what is and what ought to be that gives life its sadness; it's the difference between what we grasp for and what we reach that gives life its humour.

I've often noticed this disparity between aspiration and achievement in the case of Cedric. He is a man with a great many Grand Plans, Burning Desires, few of which come to fruition. "When the wise man points to the moon," Cedric tells me, "the fool looks at his finger." I, like Hemingway, have this inbuilt crap-detector, and whenever Cedric comes out with one of his sayings, it always swings over to the red area. Besides, Cedric's track record with members of the opposite sex is poor.

I was with him in a restaurant in Corfu—we were the only ones there—when two beautiful women came in to dine. Cedric fell in love with one of them on the spot.

"I'll ask them over to join us," I said to Cedric.

"My God, no," he said. "Where's your timing? We'll ask them to drink brandy with us, and coffee, then we'll walk through the hills, bathe in a mountain stream together and bring them back here and dance until dawn, and then. . ." He looked into the middle distance. He was thinking about the dots, I could tell.

He watched them, like a randy eagle, throughout their meal. At last, time for the brandy. He got up, walked over; as he did so, they got up to go. I heard various mutterings. Cedric returned. "She said they're a bit tired," he told me dejectedly as they went out of our restaurant. He sang the praises of the tall, auburn-haired one for the next fortnight. I still reckoned my plan—to ask them straightaway and forget the bathing, nude, in a mountain lake until we got to know their names—was much better.

"You who have aimed low in life and missed," he said when we were back home, "are—" I cut him off. It was over at red again.

It's only Cedric's strategy and tactics I don't like, not his aims. He does tend to rush relationships; most of the time he's at the After Eight mints stage when the woman's only just started on the soup, if you know what I mean. Synchronisation is *very* important. There was the time when Cedric was on the London Underground, besuited, going to a job interview. This marvellous girl sat opposite him and—*wham*—another arrow from Cupid's bow, right through Cedric's heart. He forgot about the job, got off the train when she did, and followed her through the streets of Streatham. After a mile, tiring, he approached her. "Excuse me," he said, "I'm not a sex maniac or anything like that. It's just that I've, er, fallen in love with you." She turned around, elegant, neat, hazel-eyed. "Pissorf," she said in a husky voice. When he told me, I informed him that there was a composer called Carl Orff. Was she merely introducing herself? Even Cedric, avid as he is to maintain his self-regarding sentiment, didn't believe that.

Cedric, really, is just the same as all of us—only more intense. There is in many men's—and women's—hearts a predilection to fall madly, hopelessly in love (sometimes, the worse the torment, the stronger the bond). Many of us wander through haunts of coot and hern—or Safeway supermarkets—alone, lost, incomplete, looking for that partner parcelled in Heaven but delivered to the wrong address. Some of us feel that there is a love which we perceive as through a glass darkly, or glimpse briefly as though watching a falling star move to another part of the heavens, away from our vision, out of the sight of the personal universe within each of us but still there, in the beyond, bright and shining, burning. If you ever found it, you'd never lose it, even though the person were to go away, or die, or even not love you. If you could find that one true love, then you'd love for ever, and be happy. I believe it.

I knew a man who at university loved a young woman, and she loved him. They were both religious and opted to love God rather than each other. She went into a convent, into a strict order of nuns who were not allowed to communicate with the outside world. He went into a monastery. After twenty years he decided that he'd loved her all that time, and that she was what he wanted. He left the brothers and the monastery, wrote a letter to her, smuggled it in via the gardener, returned to his lonely flat, got a job. A year later, she turned up on his doorstep. She'd always loved him, thought about him every day. They were both a bit older, of course, but that must have been quite a meeting. They built a boat together and sailed off round the world in it. That's the last I heard of them. I hope they make out, wherever they are: they certainly waited long enough for each other.

Wait a moment (you say), isn't that rather selfish? It is, in a way. I wouldn't know how to rank that kind of love alongside a priest who prays for and loves the good, the bad and the ugly, some of whom don't seem to merit much love. Spiritual love—translated into concern for others—is of a high order, and it isn't for me to decide whether it beats romantic love. I suspect that God *is* love, not an old man with a white beard and a thin, whippy rod ready to tan our hides should we transgress the rules. The only rule—and I think that those two were onto this one—is what St Augustine laid down: love and do what you will. I'm not a theologian so I can't really hold the score cards up as you all do your thing around the human ice-rink, although it does seem as if romantic love and an ordered society are largely incompatible.

Sigmund Freud makes the same point. He argues that the conflict between civilisation and sexuality is inevitable. Love is a relationship between two people, and a third can only be superfluous or disturbing; whereas civilisation and good manners are based on relationships between larger groups of people. Romantic love *is* irrational, crazy, spontaneous. It is incompatible with polite behaviour and the public good.

"When a love relationship is at its height," says Freud, "no room is left for any interest in the surrounding world; the pair of lovers are sufficient unto themselves." Most of us toe the line, rather than sailing over the blue seas to the further shores of romance. Given a chance to flee with our own true love, most of us would worry about the mortgage, or the cat's food. Would you fly with your lover by boat, train, or plane and—saying to hell with civilisation—head for the beyond? Some of us who *could* don't, while the rest of us get no offers; so the salt of poignancy is added to the pot luck of life.

The tug between inner needs and the demands of the larger society forms the basis of most classical novels and plays. If we were perfectly adjusted to our own emotional and sexual needs—or even just more honest about our passionate feelings—none of the great stories would have been written. If you're anything like me you want to shout, "Clear off, you two! Leave the rest of them to sort themselves out. Get on with it, and consummate your love." Real novelists and playwrights know it doesn't usually work like that. Perhaps it's just as well that in literature—as in life—it is so complicated; otherwise, there just wouldn't be the interest.

Nobody would go to see a *Romeo and Juliet* in which Juliet says, "R,R, wherefore art thou R?" and Romeo replies, "Can it. I've brought a ladder. Let's get the hell out of this madhouse." Few would bother to watch a *Hamlet* in which the hero says to Claudius, "Look, old chap, forget it. Let's call it an accident. I'm off behind the battlements with Ophelia." Nobody would bother to read *Tess of the d'Urbervilles* if Tess told Angel Clare that she really fancied him and he told her that the feeling was mutual and the last we see of them is disappearing towards Dorchester to shack up in a cottage or to have a dirty weekend at the Red Lion. In pulp literature, everything works out at the end. In great literature, sometimes it does, sometime it doesn't. Mostly, it doesn't: just like life.

I learned about the gap between emotional investment and return early on. In those days it wasn't sex that was at the heart of my falling in love; it was more a yearning for truth and beauty. T and B were, for me, represented by blue (or blue-grey) eyes, light brown hair, and freckled noses. To work on me, all three had to be dished up together. They were my *specific releaser*; I was crazy about that particular combination—I was *imprinted* on the powerful trio.

The whole plot of imprinting is indebted to Konrad "Baggy Trousers" Lorenz and his performing goslings. Lorenz, you'll remember, was the Austrian ethologist who took the mother goose away and walked up and down in front of the eggs when the goslings were due to come out (they imprint themselves on the first moving thing they see between twelve and twenty-four hours after hatching). As soon as they saw Konrad, that was it: he was mum. Lorenz's neighbours thought it was most odd to see his head, above the long grass at his farm, shouting, "Quack, quack." (They couldn't see the gozzies.) When the goslings became geese, they still loved Konrad, swam with him, wrapped their necks around his. They loved him. They'd been programmed to love that initial moving object just as I was programmed on blue eyes, brown hair, and freckles. It's Mother Nature—trouble-maker—up to her tricks again.

Some women are imprinted for life on their father's moustaches; a clean-shaven man will leave them cold. Other women can only love men with bald heads, or brown eyes, or long legs: they're hooked on one part of their dreamboat's physiognomy. Some men can only love women who are thin, or fat, who have blonde hair, or a round face, or small noses.

It was the Oedipus complex that was my true motivation. It wasn't until I was thirty-odd that it dawned on me that my *mother*, as well as my early girl friends, had the X factors: the blue, the brown and the freckles. That's where it had come from; I'd been imprinted on my mother from an early age. I'm glad to say that, now forty, I've shaken off this Oedipal bit and can fall in love with girls with brown eyes, blonde hair, no freckles; I can love whom I like, if I choose to love and like them. It's a tremendous freedom. Nobody really wants to be a human version of those goslings.

Then, in my youth, it was different. There was this girl who I fell in love with at thirteen—with the beloved requisite colouring—who was in the Salvation Army. I used to follow the band around every Sunday (she played the cornet, and very good she was, too), stand in the rain, worshipping her from the opposite pavement. It wasn't much of a life, but I loved her. At university I loved, deeply, another girl to whom I never spoke: my heart pounded so much when I saw her that I could never bring myself to say hello to her. Looking back, I could have done worse to go up to both and say "Quack, quack" or even "You're my mummy."

When A loves B, but B doesn't love A, it is—as you'll well know—far from jolly. One of the saddest stories I've ever read is *Un Coeur Simple* by Gustave Flaubert. It's a simple plot. Félicité, a servant girl, very good at baking bread and brushing up crumbs from the table, meets Théodore, a young blade. They only meet once; he is the one man in her life. That fateful day, he kisses her, talks of love, proposes. She yearns for love while he goes off and marries somebody else. All that happens to F, from then on in, is that she grows old with her one memory of love, and when she dies she sees not Jesus but the vision of a giant parrot above her head. The parrot, her pet, was the only thing that ever loved her and, more important, the only living creature that showed gratitude for her manifestations of love. We all have our moments: Félicité was rationed to one.

Sometimes, hopeless love does you no harm, providing that you can look upon your love as a privilege, something that may not lead anywhere, and certainly not to possession. But some of us—faced with the A loves B but B doesn't love A formula—cease to love at all. Some of us turn to the pursuit of power as a substitute for love. Others substitute work, or stamp albums or pets or possessions; they're easier to come by, but I doubt whether they can ever be anything other than a substitute for the real thing. Thomas Hardy gained a tremendous amount of literary success in his own lifetime *and* a fair amount of wealth and yet was an extremely unhappy man. He never felt loved and, along the way, he ceased to love.

It's most interesting to ponder on who—or what—people love. We had an old, old lady in our road who loved her poodle. When the dog died, she died soon after. Nobody to love. I know men who love pigeons more than their wives, women who love their motor cars far more than they love their husbands. You'd think that Shakespeare would have loved literature. Not a bit of it. He dashed off *Merry Wives* and *Hamlet* in no time at all. As a theatre manager, he had the high balcony seats to worry about—not to mention lisping boy actors. When the time was ripe, he went back to Stratford, forgot about the plays; it was somebody else who collected them all together, cared about them. Shakespeare became a burgher in his home town. It was what his mother would have wanted. He walked in the burghers' procession, and his eyes must have shone with delight at the pageantry. Did you feel, Bill the Quill, that after all these years you belonged, and that you'd done something of which mother would have been proud? Did you feel, at long last, that you were worthy of love?

Look here (I can hear you mutter at this juncture), all this stuff about Shakespeare is very interesting, but what about *me*? Here am I in 23 Acacia Avenue with two young kids and stuck with my friends into long runs round the park/granary loaves/slimming clubs/yoga classes/sauna baths/UV beds, and giving up chocolates. We're not doing it to save wear on the carpets. We're doing it to become more attractive, make it easier for somebody to hang up their passions on our particular peg. Could you (you ask) spare a thought for us, bearing in mind two rowdy children and a narcoleptic, awful wedded husband who comes to full emotional fruition only during *Match of the Day*?

I'll do my best. It isn't easy to cope with passion and a family, especially with young children. When kids come in through the door, thoughts of a sensual paradise and prolonged bodily contact with the male of your choice fly out of the window. I've had experience of that kind of thing, believe me, though—in my case—the body in question was a woman's.

I'd arranged to see this beautiful young woman in Weymouth. On the Big Day things didn't go too well. By the time the kids had had their breakfasts and I'd washed up and vacuumed the carpets, I was exhausted. It took me a good hour to decide what to wear and, having decided, I ran out to the car, jumped in and switched on. It wouldn't start. Sheer panic. Kick car. It starts. Get to W. No space in municipal car park. Find somewhere to park the brute. Get to

Smith's bookshop. She there. Don't tell her I've been up half the night with one of the children who had ear-ache. We get to my friend's house, loaned for the afternoon. We sit on the sofa and I—tired out—fall asleep in her arms. My friend, returning two hours later, thinks this is post-coital somnolence, but it's sheer fatigue, a 17 to 0 victory to the Trivial Round, the Common Task. I'd blown it.

This may reassure you that you're not the only one to make a mess of lovers' trysts, but it's hardly practical advice, so let's get down to the essentials. What you need in order to fall in love, whether single, widowed, partnered or married—don't fret, I'll deal with the added complications of extra-marital affairs in chapter 10—are to look good, feel good, and (as I've hinted) own a reliable watch and take a PhD in administration. Prince Charming, the man who perfectly complements you like the two halves of a torn piece of paper, exists all right. The trick is to meet him.

Where you meet him isn't important. Love can blossom on a sun-baked shore, or in a flower-strewn field on a roseate summer's day, at the coffee stall in the bus station at Salford, in the lift at Harrods, or walking through the streets of Wapping. The *stages* of love are important. A great many people blow it through nervousness. Never hurry it. To be successful in love you have to play your cards slowly: savour it all. That walk in the park, a meal together, holding hands, a cup of tea in a café. These everyday things, provided that you're together, can be irradiated by the glow of love. Not too much talk, too much nervous chatter. Keep your mouth closed, your heart open, *look* at each other, *touch* each other. Who needs senseless verbiage? If ennui sets in at this silent scenario, jump into some bushes to liven it up. Don't forget to drag him with you.

Have faith that the good things will happen. It's more likely to be you, rather than the gods, who will ruin it, and mainly through over-anxiety, not being relaxed, lacking confidence in just being yourself (anyone else you try to be is, by definition, utterly phoney). The Fates are writing the play; all you have to do is get on set and do your best. Don't worry about your figure/mole on left cheek/one ear lower than the other. *Just be you*. That's a must.

Somewhere (and this is your background philosophy, your major thrust) is a man with that special X factor, or combination of factors, waiting for you alone. Your job is to locate the blighter. In fairy tales, to find the Perfect Partner, the heroine puts on her glad rags and stands there until he comes over and asks her to dance. You'll have to be more dynamic than that, I'm afraid. Do find out where they're holding the latest archaeologists' or policemen's ball and, once there, ask him to dance and grapple him to your bosom with hoops of steel. Don't risk standing there all night, hoping he might come over—not after you've waited all that time to meet him.

Statistically speaking, you're more likely to meet your PP if you actually go out of the house (unless you live in a longhouse or in a semi packed to bursting point with interesting, incredibly dishy males). If you want Cupid's arrow to pierce you, it's no use staying in and doing the vacuuming. Going to the theatre/Africa/evening classes gives love a chance. Join a snorkel club/drama group/the YHA. *Do anything, but do get away from those four walls!* Cupid (another short-sighted trouble-maker) fires his arrows in some peculiar places, but even he draws the line at your kitchen sink. Canvass for the Tory or Labour party (don't take this too seriously, it only encourages them), join Friends of the Earth, or an operatic society, or a painting class. *Don't* play Cupid and ask Fred to dinner with Thelma on the grounds that they're both single and bound to like each other. That hardly solves your problem. Better to be an active participant in the Love Stakes than a spectator. Just get to places where you actually meet other adults and let that short-statured, endomorphic idiot (Cupid, not your PP, or husband) do his worst.

I used to enjoy getting people together at one time. Now, I concentrate on me. This was after a disastrous dinner party which we threw for Cedric and Pam, a truly lovely person. I should have known better. The following little scene demonstrates that when *some* people set out to be rejected, they really make a good job of it.

Place: our garden. Time: a summer's evening. Birds are singing, buds blossoming, tortoises chewing lettuces, grasshoppers chirruping away, and I'm wearing a pink shirt. A trestle table is covered with white paper, food and wine. My wife and I are seated, talking to Pam. Cedric enters, stage left, by the gooseberry bush.

ME: C, meet Pam. (*We all sit down.*)

PAM: Hello, Cedric. Nice to meet you. I hear you were at Cambridge.

C: True. I was the president of the New Testament Society. Can I squeeze you to a little jelly? (*He pours Pam some wine. As he does so, he breaks wind with tremendous force. The sky is suddenly filled with squawking, frightened birds.*)

WIFE: I've forgotten the *vol-au-vents*.

PAM: Have I seen your face somewhere else?

C: No. I always keep it here just below my head. (*Wife returns with v-au-v's, places them on table. Cedric reaches over to get one, and knocks an opened bottle of red wine over Pam's white dress.*)

ME: (*Disgusted*) Spot the bloody loony. (*Cedric goes around the table to help Pam, knocks her off chair, and falls on her.*)

C: Sorry. I used to know an awfully short-sighted girl once. Could only recognise a man when he was right on top of her. (*He gets up.*)

PAM: I'm sorry, I'll have to go in and change.

C: Tired of being a frog? (*He laughs.*) You know, Pam, when you were on the grass I could see right up your nostrils. You have lovely nostrils. I'm very keen on noses. I once met this ENT surgeon who . . . (*He lopes after her, wiping at her dress with a paper napkin, but she runs off.*)

ME: Good God, Cedric.

C: Nice girl that. I quite fancy her. I've got a shrewd suspicion that she quite fancies me, too. Just a look she gave me. I can always tell with women. Once, when I was on the Costa Brava . . .

It's too painful for me to continue. Even now, I wake up at night thinking about it. Please, is the moral, don't try to get people together. Concentrate on getting yourself together, doing your thing, pursuing your fate. That should be enough (if not too much) for any of us to be reasonably asked to cope with.

What I've noticed—returning, now, to advice and practicalities—is that the women who get most out of love are those who (a) are good at administration and (b) seize upon the fact that most people, including men, are appallingly shy. She who expresses interest in something that he's good at (even if it's only knitting ties, or walking), gets him talking about himself (that's a subject that many of us feel easiest with), and isn't afraid to go up and introduce herself to those more interesting men is doing something about her own shyness, and his. A smile, a word (usually "hello") has started off many an earth-shattering, passionate relationship or (damn) a sincere friendship. A smile is a powerful signal; the word "hello" is as good a start as any. I notice that Cedric *never* says hello to people. He's always thinking about the dots, or himself.

A word here to those who ask, *Can love survive marriage?* Cedric reckons it can't; I think it can, but that the flames of passion have to be fanned more than a little. Assuming that you don't just stand around all day like a Dresden porcelain shepherdess, and that you love your partner and want him to love you too, how do you get over the fact that he might catch a glimpse of you in the kitchen, or—Heaven forbid—in your rollers *and* slippers. There's companionship love, and there's passion. We need both in our lives, but can we have both within marriage, with the same person? To dare is the answer. To hell with the question.

Assuming that you give your partner room to grow, never become life-denying, and never renege on your own deeply felt need for romantic love in your life, quite a lot is possible. You may be married to the same man for fifty or sixty years; that's a hell of a long time, but it doesn't mean romance has to go after the first six months. Quite a few people do better than that. Some still love each other, romantically, after all those years. *That*, I must admit, is something that impresses me and does me good to see.

My mother tells me that when she was young she was courted by a coalman called Percy. "He never married," she said. "Loved only me. Told me that if he couldn't have me, he didn't want anybody else." I hope you have an equivalent of Percy in your life, even if you have central heating. That kind of distant love—the hopelessness of the heart's affections—we all know about. But how do you kindle, and keep going, the flames of passion with somebody you actually live with?

I'll deal with this problem more fully in the chapter on family life. For those who are desperate to know, it's enough to say here that Little Things Mean A Lot: an unexpected bunch of flowers, a stolen kiss when you're visiting friends, a cuddle in the kitchen while you're waiting for the kettle to boil—why waste precious moments? An old lady told me that she liked her husband because he always held her hand at the tram stop and when they went walking on a Sunday. "I like holding hands," she said. "It shows you like each other." Washing up when it's not your turn, having a meal—which you can't really afford—in a restaurant together, saying "I think you're marvellous." Things like these make all the difference.

So does having a sense of fun. Have a dirty weekend together somewhere ridiculous like Chipping Sodbury or Blackpool; make love in a field, or in the kitchen while terrified that your mother will pop her head around the door; rub his back with a soapy loofah, let him rub yours, while you're in the bath together; walk in the rain; throw a ball to each other in the park; feed the ducks. Marriage can be fun; it doesn't have to be a life sentence without remission or parole. We'll get back, I promise, to this vital topic after the bits on love and sex. They *don't* stop with that walk up the aisle or the trip to the registry office. There *can* be life after marriage.

We all have to learn—men as well as women—to be much more open and honest about our feelings, our hang-ups, our confusions. We all have to learn to love a whole lot better. Why fear it? Love is the one waveband into which we all must tune, the insistent drumbeat to which we all must march, if we are to become that person who is the truest and best self. We can tune in to love by loving another adult, by loving a child, and also through art, religion, philosophy, dance, music, drama, and play (ie, having fun). Great love stories and great music reach our unconscious minds and tell us something that we know to be true: there is a Great Principle of Love in the universe. I never denigrate love, whatever kind it is. If I see a nun who loves Jesus, a priest who loves God, I respect them for the fact that they have devoted their lives to Love.

I respect mad, irrational—even carnal—love, too. Carol has told me, more than once, "I need boom-boom, knickers-to-the-wind, crazy, vulnerable, passionate love. I need a man to shave my legs for." I know what she means, and I don't denigrate it. We all need to love and be loved. A friend told me that she was having lunch with a dishy man; it was at a conference and there wasn't much on the programme that afternoon. "Why don't we go to bed together?" asked my friend, over coffee. They did. I was rather shocked at that. I mean, they hardly knew each other. "What was it like?" I asked (nosey old me). "Lovely," she said. "The funny thing was I forgot to ask him his first name." I suppose that instant attraction when consummated so openly *is* rather shocking. Personally (given that neither of the partners had spots or VD), I think my primary emotion, on reflection, was jealousy. There's no moral judgement I can make on my pal, it's her body after all. That afternoon she wasn't looking for love, she was looking for carnality. It happens (or rather, doesn't) to us all. Did I hear somebody at the back say worse luck? That's what I thought.

As we go through the 'Eighties I hope that men will come off the silly, destructive, Tarzan/Jane, Popeye/Olive dichotomies and feel able to express their emotions more freely. Biceps, I hope, will be out, feelings, in. There will continue to be blurring of the sex roles, and this can lead to better love lives for us all. We don't (or, at least, *I* don't) want to see over-petulent, fussy, weepy, irrational, vain, hysterical men; nor do we want to see butch, strident, over-aggressive, bossy, cold women. Men will learn to laugh, to cry, to be sad, to be joyful, to show compassionate feelings, to love; women will learn to fight for their rights and to be loving, too. Carol is no slouch when it comes to the women's movement. Yet she readily acknowledges the need for the irrational, for LOVE, in her life.

Who needs tough men? Who wants women who are insensitive, bullying, paranoid, with muscles like brewers' draymen and the sexual aura of Brillo pads? I want women who address themselves to the tasks of life (love, friendship, work) with confidence in their own identity, with sympathy and empathy, with non-stereotyped social relationships, and with an understanding that feelings, sensitivity and intuition can be combined with intelligence, social drive and emotional toughness—*and* integrity for the good of their partners and for the good of the whole community. What do I want for men? I want exactly the same thing. Please, no more of that me tough man/you helpless woman dichotomy. It doesn't help people to grow. It doesn't help people to love each other.

Once we learn to be the person that we really are, other things fall into place. Take passion. It provides, for a time (limited, mostly), joy, hate, excitement, despair. My advice? Wallow in it, for like the warm weather it passeth; you may wake up one morning and wonder what all the fuss was about. The fuss was about you having a glimpse of The Big One; like the Old Man of the Sea, you knew you had it there on the end of the line, you lashed yourself to the mast, but you couldn't bring the wretched thing back to shore. Who cares? For a while, it was yours: the one you'd waited for, the one that makes it all worthwhile. "Love is like the measles," said Jerome K Jerome. "We all have to go through it." Oh, no, it isn't. It's much more than that. It's a glimpse of the enchanted garden, it's the knowledge that one may be destroyed but not defeated—not when one loves. The OM of the S knew that, and we must know that, too.

Human beings are the only creatures on earth who have the power to step outside themselves, look at themselves, with humour, with disgust, with self-respect, with suspicion. Many of us are "split-off" from our own unconscious, from the collective unconscious, and also from the magic of the night sky and the beauty of Nature. In love, we regain ourselves, our hearts beat in tune with the earth.

Just a minute (you say), love is marvellous, but couldn't we be just a little bit more hard-headed and realistic about this? Can't love also be used to manipulate, control, psychologically smash, damage, and humiliate other human beings? Of course it can. The only antidote to that is to insist on space, growth—*but allow your partner the same things.*

Love is a privilege, not a possession. You decide to love, or be loved; if you feel that the love to which you have made yourself vulnerable will destroy you, then you must make your own choice. Life is nothing more than a series of problems to be solved; it's an uneasy business—it never stays still. We have to grow, to change, and as we change, our passions, emotions, and yearnings are involved, as well as our reason. If you want passion badly enough, you'll pay the price. Whether you can afford to is up to you. In the 'Eighties, I hope we'll all take more responsibility for our own decisions: we'll negotiate about feelings, about who cooks the supper, about whether it's a good idea to go to North Wales with Julian and live in a tepee. In the middle of this honesty, this negotiation we will—above all—*take responsibility for ourselves.*

Look (you insist), I'm *for* love: it's just that my partner wears his vest, shirt *and* underpants in bed and is more into billiards and a quick grapple on the sofa than romance. Where does your notion of love stand in the face of that? I stand by what I've said. Some men appear to be extremely unpromising material, but they can be taught. You must teach your man to look upon you as a sunset, a walk through a country lane, a rippling brook—rather than a pair of tits on legs. I once met a sailor on a train; we spoke of our respective girl friends (this was some time ago). "Mind you," he said, "*all* women are marvellous." You must get that concept across, teach your man not to waste you, or your time, and to make you immortal with lots of big kisses. I know a woman who insisted that her man write poetry to her; her point—and it was a good one—was that she was worth it. "We'll buy a giant bed and while the Nightingale toots," he wrote to her from Barnsley, on an Away Day ticket, "make mad, passionate love." Not bad. At least he didn't force the rhyme ("In my shirt, pants, and boots"?).

Men are, with respect to love, rather like dogs. Train them right, as puppies, and you get a better response when they're bigger. *Say* what you want. Don't let him get away with the odd box of chocolates as a trade-off for watching *Match of the Day* without you running your fingers through his hair and breathing heavily. Insist that it's your right to breathe heavily; train him to respond to your signals. Why should you settle for second-best? You have, basically, the same material as Cleopatra, Venus, Eve, and Lady Hamilton—they were women for whom their men would switch off Liverpool *v* Tottenham. Why be Josephine? With men, if you settle for the third-rate, you'll find that they dish it up the whole time. You are worth first-rate, so start training him now.

One more urgent issue: the platonic notion of love. Is it possible to have a platonic relationship with a person of the opposite sex? Not only is it possible, but the whole notion of *friendship* between men and women is absolutely vital and will become more and more important as we get to know each other a little more in the years to come. Friendship is a house with many windows. Without my lovely friend Gwen, my dear friend Carol, without Beth, Amy, Judy and Jenny, not to mention others—my life would be greatly diminished. I think I've made my views on this fairly clear, but it's worth saying again that the opposite sex make up half the world. Why, among the many people in that half, shouldn't some of them be our best friends? What a lot of fun men are missing who have no women as close friends! What a lot of insight into male psychology women are missing if the only relationships they have with men are in factory and kitchen, office and living room, or boardroom and bedroom. Some of my best friends are women (no, I'm not being funny) and I love them, not in a physical, passionate way, but I do love them and I always will.

Back now to the girl I called Tess. We left her, emotionally speaking, with Fenchurch Street, while her parents held Park Lane and Mayfair, plus one hotel. She was losing. Tess had nowhere to go, no one who really loved her (if only people would love each other more), nowhere to belong. I'd like to tell you that I solved the whole thing. I didn't. They put her into care and protection. Me, I'd have sent the parents. I loved Tess, in my way, within the rules, but her parents didn't, and that's the big one. They didn't know that the greatest gift you can give to a child is happiness, that you have to be happy, you have to try to give it. They'll carry that with them. If you're not happy, tell your children about it. Tell them how you wanted happiness too, but didn't find it. They'll understand, and forgive. If you can, say the pain stops here, with me. I'm not going to pass it on to you. That's the most generous, the most marvellous, the most loving gift of all.

I explained to Tess that sometimes young people have to play the parts of adults. They have to learn to see parents as people, and to forgive. She came out of care after a year and went home. She could stand it now, see that they'd never change. It was she who had to change, grow, live her life. She got a boyfriend; he was nice, and that helped. I was a little jealous of him. I was very fond of Tess. She's married now, to someone she loves, and has two little children. She sends me a Christmas card every year, which I cherish because Tess is a person who had no love herself, but learned to love; she got it from somewhere. Her name, by the way, wasn't Tess.

Steps towards the magic garden of love

○ *Do something crazy and romantic once a month (or once a week if time's not on your side).* I saw this friend, Wendy, at the other end of the aisle in our supermarket. Few people about. I picked up the long packet of Italian spaghetti and did my Fred Astaire bit. I twirled and wove my way towards her. Close up, I growled, "Dwarling, kiss me." It wasn't Wendy. What the hell? It's the principle of the thing that counts and I'm sure, with practice, you can do better than that.

○ *There's a taboo on tenderness in our society. Ignore it.* What's the point in loving people if you never express it? Touching, cuddling, walking with your arms around each other, the quick hug in the bathroom are all the outward show of love. Insist on getting your share. With kids, we know that if you have 'em, you should love 'em. I think it's the same—or should be—for adults.

○ *Don't split off love from your ordinary life, where you are now. Love should be where you are.* I knew a woman who had been married for years; and for years she has loved dearly a man whom she sees once a month, a man somewhere else. That may be practical, convenient, manageable. I can't help thinking it's also very dishonest.

○ *Accept the disappointments of love, and have a sense of humour about them.* This couple married. He'd bought a house, secretly. He wanted her first to see it as a bride; he'd carry her over their threshold—there they'd build their nest. When she *did* see it, that hopeful, blushing bride burst into tears: it was such a run-down, dilapidated old place. She never got over the house thing and left him a year later. He'd have done better to give her a rose and take her on the back of a horse to an estate agent. She'd have done better to see the funny side of things.

○ *Believe in love and get in there where people are, where love is.* Don't stay at home with your slushy romance—or the TV—and get it all second-hand. Somebody told me that however bad television is, it's never as bad as life; I'd say that no matter how bad life is, it's better than watching TV. Life is people, not electronics—or even print. Even I, a print addict, realise that.

○ *Be bold.* Cedric is bold, though he's often rebuffed. "Would you like to kiss me?" he asked an African girl at a party. "It's bad enough being black," she said. What's amazing is the number of women who *don't* rebuff Cedric, who agree with his claim that kissing transmits the Life Force and that if you kiss enough, you'll live until you're ninety. If Cedric, who is to love and romance as Cyril Smith is to ice-skating, is in there with a chance, there must be hope for you.

○ *Learn to love more.* Love isn't possession, suffocation, ownership. To love somebody is (or should be) a privilege. Be open to love, even though, sometimes, it feels as though you've been hit on the back of the neck with a baseball bat. I'm sure when you're old and two foot shorter, you'll agree with the chap (Tennyson, was it?) who said, " 'Tis better to have loved and lost/Than never to have loved at all."

○ *No more excuses.* Don't use your mother/early childhood/family commitments/dodgy ankle/lack of height/excess of height as an excuse for not loving. The world is full of people looking in the mirror, worrying about themselves. It's also full of warm, sensitive people—just like you. Give yourself a 6000-mile service this week and get out and meet them.

○ *Aim for friendship.* The more friends you have, of *both* sexes, the more likely you are to meet that special man moulded just for you. To like people, mix with them, say that first "hello", is a very good way to travel. At least you're in the general target area as far as Cupid is concerned.

○ *Don't be stingy with your love.* Don't ration love, as though you were afraid of running out of it. There's a vast reservoir of love inside us all, so why dish it out in tiny cupfuls? Love. Dare. Live. Take a chance. We may have less time than we think.

Make love, not sex

In The Pure Drop, Tony—this fiftyish friend of mine whose one claim to fame is that his whole body is covered in enough black, springy hair to supply a sofa factory—was going on about sex. (It's either that, darts, or football.) His passion is stocking tops. "Remember that bare expanse of thigh?" he asked. I did. "Tights spoilt all that." He started telling me about the women's legs he'd groped as a young man. Tony's into feeling all right, but it's nothing to do with women as real people. It's a pity that women aren't articulated, like lorries. "You know the bit I want," Tony could shout up to his wife in the evening. "Throw it down."

Old Charlie comes in next, staggering towards the bar, tongue hanging out, like T E Lawrence heading for Aqaba. He joins us.

"Where've you bin, then?" asks Tony. "On the bed with the missus, if you'd like to know. It takes us old uns longer but I don't begrudge the time. Sex keeps you young." It does and, whether it's profane or sacred, sad or joyous, ridiculous or deeply moving, it assuredly never lacks interest.

For good sex you need a pleasant setting, plenty of time, lots of space, mutual attraction, and a common goal. You also need tenderness (preferably love), plus peace of mind. The P of M isn't always easy to achieve. The Rigours of Life (we'll come across *them*, again) have to be contended with, especially if you're married. I mean, the reason that you'd rather have a nice piece of toast than sex (you could argue) is that you're always tired/aware of the kids/put off by him not taking his vest (socks? boots?) off/afraid that his mother (or worse, your mother) will come through the door just as he's kissing you behind the aspidistra. I know, I know. There's often a tremendous gap between Ideal and Reality, theory and practice. What (you query) happened to those trains rushing through tunnels, waves crashing on rocks, arrows thudding into cider barrels and lovers disappearing into the foam?

Besides the Rs of L, most women, if they want sex, have to cope with men. Though it seems churlish to say so, on the sexual ice-rink many men score 3.5 for presentation and 2.5 for content. Men have been taught to be tough, hide their feelings, never admit to having any emotions. Some men don't cry (or jump for joy, shout out loud, bubble with excitement—unless, of course, they're watching Man Utd). Men—a lot of them—are into work, acquisition, status. They dream of winning, even with sex. This is the "great stud" fantasy, the pathetic "phallusy", the notion that sex is about winning. "He's after my body, not my mind." Just as well, really; he'd soon find out that you know damn all about Bristol FC.

Most women know that sex involves, or should involve, holding, looking, stroking, whispering, kissing, hearing, feeling, waiting, tasting, gently touching, hugging—two hearts beating as one. Some men find this kind of thing very difficult. They're not into tenderness. On the emotional side of things (and emotions are the things that move us, provide the power in the boiler-house), men tend to still be at the L-plate stage. "I'm tender," you cry. Good old you. You're still not home though, as far as sex is concerned. Your problem is to find a man who isn't primarily into the job, cars, the local barmaid's tits—and who can sustain a pleasant conversation for more than ten minutes. Men, let's face it, can be terribly boring.

You see, men see life in terms of a pecking order; it's hard for them to handle equality. I go to a local sports centre regularly to use the Multigym machine (pit your muscles against me: improve). Men are happy there. There is a pectoral order. King of the Gym is a quiet black guy, muscles like footballs all over his body. It's safe; there are standards to be attained; nobody talks. Same when I go fishing. The skill of each man is sussed out, a leader emerges, anyone who talks about anything other than fish is immediately suspect. A man has to get his school report from his mates: he has to know that Charlie's C, he's B, and Harry, over there, is A for Ace. Just like in school.

This competitive attitude doesn't lend itself to emotional intimacy, or to good sex. With many men, feelings are nowhere. I've hardly ever spoken to another man about my feelings. It's the setbacks—and the triumphs—of the *deed*, not of the heart, that we talk about. I've never spoken to a man about happiness, misery, hopelessness, joyousness, sadness, love. They're quite important, really—as important as muscles, or fish. I couldn't say to a man, "Don't you think most people live out their lives in a kind of quiet desperation?" He'd think I'd gone off my trolley. I could say that to a woman—she'd know what I'm talking about. Potentially, many, many women can respond to the drum beats of their own hearts. They could dance all right, if there weren't so many partners wearing spiritual and emotional lead-lined boots. Sex is a whole orchestra. Why play the tune with a spoon and a bottle?

To illustrate the difference in the psychology of the female and the male, I think it's timely to quote Case 1: Salome and the Grapefruits. In this one-acter, Salome is played by Gertrude, aged eleven. The place is a small council house in the North. The time is the Second World War, during which contest (as a handful of you will know) there was a severe shortage of citrus fruit. At ten each Thursday morning, Gertie would open her back door to a motley collection of small boys. They were ushered into the living room, asked to sit on the floor. Gertie's mother, while this was going on, was working in the local munitions factory. There was no demand, then, for "cake-icing" women who played the role of housewife.

G was doing her bit to beat Hitler. If we boys aged between five and eleven had to go to the war later, at least we'd have our memories. We could walk up the Golden Staircase to Paradise with one Good Time in our knapsacks. Something like that. Or it could have been that Gertie just liked dancing in the nude. Perhaps she saw herself as a skinnier version of Pavlova transmitting some of the beauty of art, and the ecstacy within her, to a dull world. Who knows? Times were hard, then. There were no life-size dolls, strip shows, girlie mags, sex films, or sexual aids to keep us men amused, though there *were* sepia-toned photographs of women and men "doing it" in which the latter kept their socks on.

We were less afraid of women in those days—merely thought them a bit peculiar, odd, not interested in fighting. At least we weren't quite as afraid of women as men are now. We'd never heard of the castration complex; didn't fear that women, if treated as real people, would do something awfully nasty. We just thought that women—or, in our case, girls—had a different set of interests and values than men do. And they have.

My job, as everybody sat around on the carpet, was to wind up the gramophone at the far end of the room, make sure everything was in working order, a record ready. Usually we started off with *The Egyptian Ballet* followed by Bing Crosby's *White Christmas* and worked up via *The Entrance of the Little Fawn* to the finale, Ravel's *Bolero*—as I remember, a fast-moving piece. I'd stand by with the little tin of "Embassy" gramophone needles, medium tone, use each needle ONCE only, guaranteed. G would give me the signal, I'd open up the wooden doors of the hand-cranked instrument, and Gertie would move about the room waving her arms, and slowly undulating her upper body in front of the assembly of boys. Gertrude lacked a bosom, but not grit.

I want now to mention the existential gap, the misunderstanding, the psychic rift that existed between Gertie and her audience. The only way we could explain it then was to postulate that G might be slightly odd. Most of us just accepted it as part of the rich pageantry of life and anyway we had our own reasons for being there every week. Raggedy trouser'd we were; philanthropists we were not. At the end of the performance Gertie would give each boy a grapefruit. Vitamin C deficiency, or sheer greed, the joy of getting something for nothing, was absolutely rampant in that dark era. As Gertie circled around the room, many's the young eye glassed over only waiting for the performance to stop—Gertie was painfully thin, and with skin like the white notes on a piano—so that the best bit could arrive: the distribution of the citrus fruit that Gertie's father, a sailor in the Merchant Marine, had brought home from overseas.

It took me a long time to figure the motives of everybody concerned in these theatricals. Gertie, I think, was trained in the old school: she just wanted to give, and to be appreciated. We boys, trained in another school, wanted a free lesson in anatomy and—more important, since one soon got the anatomical picture, so to speak—free grapefruits. The youngest boy there even had the cheek to say to me once, in a high, whingey voice, "I wish they were oranges." I found the sight of Gertrude in the nude all rather reassuring: my first inkling of the fact that it is an imperfect world, that women are keen on getting together and enjoying themselves while men have constantly in mind the question, *what am I getting out of this?*

Basically, men want pornography and chips. G knew this. She gave us boys the wartime equivalent. It was a pity her mother ever found out about the shows and put a stop to them. There had been a noticeable improvement in the skin tone of the lads of the neighbourhood. This is more than can be said of Gertie and her spotty face, pitiful body, ribs sticking out like an accordion keyboard, looking out of the living room window as, to the tremendous climax of *Bolero,* she threw her torn knickers to the ceiling. After the shows, we boys never included Gertrude in any of our games. That's what happens, I guess, to women who see their role as simply to entertain and to feed men. Men, served thus, do not even think of giving the woman a quick round of applause, never mind a word of praise, a kiss. At least I helped with the gramophone. MORAL: *If you dance nude for your husband or whatever, including feeding him, make sure that you're getting something worthwhile in return. Don't offer pearls to MCPs: it only encourages them.*

I'm rabbiting on about the psychology of men—and their need to win—because, with sex, it's much better if you feel close to someone (unless you're performing in a local strip club). The feeling of closeness, of unity, leads on to good—sexual—things. After all, if he's clumsy (most men are) but sensitive, you can always tell him what to do (or, if the worst comes to the worst, draw a diagram). It's when your man has an emotional quotient, an EQ, of 49—when he can't express his feelings, when he can't tell you about what's going on inside him—that it's much more difficult.

It's interesting that one of the boys at Gertie's shows was my best pal. At sixteen, he told me (I'd known him since I was four) that his mother wasn't his mother, his "sister" was! She was years older than he, a grown woman. She had, apparently, been seduced by the butcher. Not that that made much difference to me. I was hurt he hadn't told me before. I was his mate, his friend, his real buddy. More recently, a friend smashed up his house, his wife, his car, his life. We'd been drinking in the same pub, chatting for months about this and that. He didn't mention anything about stress at home to me. Men don't. They find it hard to converse about things which are really vital, in some cases life and death to them. It's the male, taciturn, All-Action Show—not a lot gets said—that makes closeness rather hard to come by.

Women are much better at relationships, but they have their own problems. They're brought up to behave nicely, talk nicely, be polite, not to be aggressive. I have this theory that bottled-up aggression lies at the root of a great deal of mental illness, especially among women—and it's women who are at risk in middle life from anxiety, depression, feelings of unreality. I think it's the repressed anger of girls and young women which wreaks such tremendous emotional havoc at a later stage in the journey towards maturity, oneness. I know plenty of women—once vibrant, alive—who are presently living out their lives the Valium way or who've ended up as short-term (and, with one or two, long-term) patients in a mental hospital. Little girls are taught not to play rough games. That's not much of a preparation for living in the real world. Life is sometimes very rough indeed.

Little girls are by nature gentle, passive. Women are the weaker sex. Whoever promulgates this crap? Whoever believes this rubbish? Women, on average, live longer than men. They're much tougher than men, emotionally (and that's what counts; these days, who needs muscles?). Women seem to be able to make friendships more easily than men. What have we done to women that makes so many of them unhappy, depressed *in spite of their emotional resilience?* It must be something pretty powerful to produce that kind of effect. And who has done it? Could it be—you've guessed—men? What I'm told in the psychology books and in the media about the nature of girls and women just doesn't check with my own experiences with them, as people. There's something odd about it all. What's going on? It's important to know. You can't have good sex unless you relate to your partner as a real person and throw all those fantasies about women, and men, out of the nearest window.

Let's cheer ourselves up a bit by having a look at a real woman—or, at least, a real girl—I once knew called Marjorie. She knew what she wanted, did Marje, and what she wanted was SEX.

Marjorie told me, one sunny morning while I was sitting on our pavement rolling little balls of tar in my fingers (but thinking all the time, you understand), how men and women actually did it. It was usual for the man, said Marje, to lie on top of the woman; dogs don't do that because their legs get in the way. Also, said Marjorie, mysteriously, the man has to get the woman worked up by kissing her a lot. This kind of conversation, with plenty of detail to follow, beats rolling tar any day. I was about nine at the time, Marje was eleven (is this a critical time in women's lives?). I was happy to receive sex education from an older woman with this kind of gritty, no-nonsense approach.

The first time I kissed Marje was in the Gaumont watching *They Died With Their Boots On.* The Indians had just started to attack the cavalry when Marje (who liked love bits, not fighting bits; with me it was the opposite) flung herself on me, pressing her lips to mine. "Get me worked up," she said. "I . . . I . . . I . . ." This must be very like drowning. Marjorie was quite a big girl, while I was more compact, though with plenty of courage. I couldn't help feeling, as Marje sprang at me whenever an Indian looked over a hill, if this is sex, give me a horse, a gun and a Sixth Cavalry charge.

Marje said she loved me after the Gaumont episode; her love took the form of springing out on me whenever I walked past her hedge. Everything's like something and this was like a barrage balloon suddenly falling out of the sky on to your head—a BB with lips. "I love you," Marge would say. "Get me worked up," she'd shout. "I . . . I . . . I . . . My mother . . . If she . . ." *Swoosh.* Those lips would descend on mine. I'd lean on her gate to get my breath back, and she'd insist on holding my hand as I gulped in fresh air. Pale hands I loved beside the Shalimar—where are you now, Marje, and did you ever find anybody that could hold their breath long enough to get you going? I began to see the attraction of stamp albums: they don't jump on you and stick a mouth like an animated sink plunger over your tiny puckered lips.

For her part, Marje persevered. She jumped out at me from shop doorways, coming home from school, and from the hut in the park. She pinned me against the lamp-post at the top of the road. She kissed me once as I emerged from the front door. I staggered back in to my stamps. I won't bore you with this. "You're afraid of your mother," Marge told me one day, and packed me in. She went out with a boy of fourteen, an hirsute youth, much more suitable. She'd sussed me out as a shrimshanker who disappeared when things got too hot; I was a lazy blighter who'd do anything but grasp the nettle.

I realised early on that women could be hunters—thrusting, if not slightly pushy. The girls I knew in the road bore no relationship to the girls I'd read about in those reading primers, the candy-floss bunch. Marje was tough, honest and, despite her over-enthusiasm, highly attractive. She didn't resort to strategies of deception, play the feak and weeble woman, manoeuvre men from a position of weakness. It was the men who were weak. They weren't in the same league. It was men who were (and are?) so disappointing. Marjorie knew it: men lack stamina.

Some women don't know it. Some women treat men as though they really were Tarzan. At least, Tarzan could swing through trees (though his conversation wasn't marvellous). There are some women who exercise, as Oscar Wilde put it, "the worst form of tyranny the world has ever known. The tyranny of the weak over the strong." There we go again. Men strong? Women weak? If you believe that, you'd believe anything. Some women do believe it. They manipulate, whine, moan, bitch, emotionally blackmail and negotiate from a position of weakness simply because it saves hassle, enables them to avoid making any decisions about themselves, absolves them from facing up to themselves and their own reality. What a way to go. Playing the Servant Girl, the Invalid, to some oaf of a man because you don't have the courage to say, "This won't do." I can only assume that these deceptive strategies confer the dubious advantage of the power behind the home never having to stand up and say, "I'm me."

What's it all about? Real relationships. Love. Treating each other as people. Sex taking place between equals in a caring, honest context. Sex between Slave and Master is no good. When Brute Man and Cake-Icing Lady run towards each other on that beach, waves gently lapping the shore, the results are likely to be not love on the sands but disaster. When a woman meets a man—as things stand—it's as well to put your money on pathos, jealousy, misunderstanding, fear, mistrust, and envy. A man and a woman meet, face to face, but there's a vast psychic rift between them. That's not a good augury for those trains, tunnels, arrows, and barrels I've mentioned.

When women stop training their daughters to be subservient and self-effacing, we'll be in with a chance. When fathers (and mothers) stop training their sons to be aggressive, brash, ashamed of their own feelings of tenderness, we'll be able—men and women—to get close to each other. Assume that the couple running across the beach actually get to each other (and that the man hasn't been distracted by an angler casting for bass). Assume that the woman, open-hearted, affectionate, says to the man, "Do what you will." She may very well find herself in a snorkel mask, washing his dishes, or being taken on a 92 bus to see the Arsenal. Women and men approach each other as strangers. The vast majority of us can't have good sex with a stranger.

Mind you, I don't think it helps if women, in the face of men's brutalised attitude towards feelings, become too brash themselves. For one thing, where many men are already terrified of women, this is going to make men escape even deeper into their own macho hide-outs. For another, I think the last thing that women should imitate is men. If women become like men, the world will be a very bleak place indeed, if it lasts. The tendernesses, I'm arguing, have to be *shared*, not thrown overboard in despair. Women have to develop their own inborn crap-detectors, be more straight, say it how it is, for them. They want equality with men, and that's fair. It doesn't mean that women have to be macho. If it goes that way then sex, like life, will become increasingly nasty, brutish, and short.

I once had to visit a remand home for naughty girls. I gave them reading tests, measured their IQs, that sort of thing. One girl came in and stripped off to her pants and bra. "Goin' to examine me?" she asked. I shuffled nervously. "Clothes on, ducks," I said. "Come and do the coloured blocks." She was most disappointed. Recently, I had a blind date with a very liberated lady. She'd written to me and I—crazy, romantic fool—agreed to meet. Little country pub, goodish conversation—next minute she asks the landlord if we can have a room. I say . . . I'm against rushed sex, as I've mentioned. In room, she undresses, approaches me from behind, says, "Stick your tongue in my ear." Very difficult. No coloured blocks with me. What was I to do? This was Keystone Kops stuff, not my style. I explained my point of view. She dressed. We chatted. We parted, friends, I think.

Pity, that. When I was a teenager and into sex in the head, I'd often fantasised about a woman nude on a bed, crooning, "I'm yours" as I moved forward, taking off my tie. When it happened I wasn't ready for it or, perhaps, had moved past it. Wrong place. Wrong time. Uncertain whether the partner was right or wrong. All in all, in that kind of situation—and I didn't really feel *easy* in that bedroom—I've found that I'm better off with my phrenology books, or filing my nails under N. I can see the problem that women have: if they take the initiative in sex, usurp the man's (self-allocated) role as the leader, then Tarzan creeps back to his treehouse (more shaken than stirred) and starts looking at his train set.

On the other hand (isn't life fraught?), men are past masters at rushing things sexually. I remember Cedric telling me about this woman he'd seduced (was she short-sighted? I find the thought of somebody doing it with Cedric quite revolting) and, as a finale, had opened a bottle of champagne and swooshed the bubbles over her breasts. That's quite imaginative for Cedric. The next time he met her, he had two bottles of champagne ready (he always overdoes things) and squirted the bubbly over her *before* the finale—while she was undressing, in fact. She wasn't too happy about it. Her dress—and the duvet—got soaked, and she refused to consummate the reunion. I should think that champagne, of whatever vintage, is no compensation for seeing Cedric, nude, in his socks, chasing you around the bedroom. Enthusiasm, to be effective, has to be combined with finesse.

The solution to these little misunderstandings between the sexes is more honest—and, of course, *equal*—negotiation. If your man is to sex what Genghis Khan was to ballet, tell him (your man, not GK) what it is you want, before you start, and as you go along. If you don't like him in the nude save for his vest and navy-blue woollen hat, tell *him*, not me or your best friend. It's your body, your sex life. You're not there, I hope, in a servicing role, but nobody minds being a remedial teacher if the results are gratifying.

Anybody who's married, as I've indicated, has a great deal of difficulty in finding time (and a place) to be tender in. Even if the children are at Sunday School, who's to say that the very tidy lady from next door won't come in just as you and your husband have managed to climb into bed, or into a large plastic bin-liner (some people are branching out, sexually). Nothing's more likely to put you off than a haughty voice shouting upstairs, "Can I have my lawnmower/barbecue/punch bowl back?" This can be very off-putting. Privacy, when you're living with children about the place, is particularly difficult to find.

I remember, a few years ago, going inside one of those curious sex shops in Soho. I bought a vibrator, just to show willing. On the train home I met a friend. He kept staring at the parcel on my knee. I then realised that through the thin, brown paper it was possible to see the words "personal vibrator", in large red letters. I hurriedly turned the parcel over. Same message. I laughed, too loudly. "For making patterns in cake icing," I said. It was the best I could do.

That night I told my wife what I'd secreted in the wardrobe. "Get it out," she said, in her practical way. I did, jumped into bed, and switched the thing on. It promptly emitted a loud whirring noise like a fan heater.

"Turn that bloody Black and Decker down," shouted my son, "I'm trying to do my homework." The eldest yelled that it was about time that we put up shelves in the bedroom. The youngest, in the adjoining room, shouted, "Do you have to vacuum the carpet at night?" I switched off.

"Women like men with imagination," my wife said, "but this is ridiculous." I fell asleep wondering about the possibility of booking a room for a fortnight in the local isolation hospital.

Worse was to come. At breakfast, the younger daughter appeared with the V held aloft. "What's this?" she asked. "For planting potatoes," I said. "For making marks on pottery," said my wife. We both turned down the suggestion that the YD take the vibrator into school to show it to the art mistress. I hid the V in the vase in the hall on my way to the bathroom. The last thing I wanted at that time of day was *Gardener's Question Time*, or my daughter saying that she felt quite sure that the art mistress would find a use for it.

That evening I was standing at the kitchen sink, wiping a few dishes, when I noticed a small but happy band of children—supervised by the YD—making holes in the potato patch with something that looked remarkably like a pink banana. "The Woodentops have found it," I yelled to the wife. "They're doing a spot of digging." My spouse tells me to play it cool so, when the children have gone, I go out and rescue the offending instrument, clean it, put it in a drawer marked "passports and medical cards". When the children were in bed I came up with a Bright Idea.

"Do you think," I asked, "if I went back to the shop they'd swop the vibrator, little used, for a blow-up inflatable woman? The kids would have a hell of a time with that." My wife put down *The Guardian*. "Think of the neighbours," she said. Next day I went to have a cup of coffee with Carol, and told her of the problem. "A fiver's a fiver," said Carol. "Perhaps you could use it as a whisk—instant puddings and things. Or Sellotape it on to your toothbrush. It seems a pity to waste it." The vibrator is still in the house—in the inside pocket of my dinner jacket. Let's hope that the next time I'm asked to talk to the Soroptimists, I don't pull it out and attempt to smoke it. MORAL: *Don't try to have sex with children about.* Get somebody to mind them, or—if you can—have a dirty weekend in Brighton. Hotel bedrooms are a great aphrodisiac.

What am I trying to prove? Mainly, that although there is no longer a taboo on sex in our society, there is a *taboo on tenderness*; there is also too little emphasis on feelings, as opposed to the mechanics of sex. Of course, be honest with young children: give it to them straight, when they ask. By all means let's have sex education in school, but don't disguise it as "religious studies" and don't forget to teach boys as well as girls. ("My lads don't get pregnant," one bright spark of a secondary school headmaster said to me, turning down the offer of sex education for his pupils.) In the past we've been repressive, hypocritical; we mustn't rush to the other extreme and encourage youngsters to be sexually active, if they're not emotionally ready for sex.

Young people, these days, have choice. In the old days it was a Girdles and Confetti morality; a young woman wouldn't usually take her girdle off unless you were legally wed. (To get one of those things off you needed a whole day and a pair of wire cutters.) Now young people can choose whether to live together, sleep together, before marriage. It should be a choice based on knowledge of the facts: the financial, social and emotional considerations involved. Some couples will argue that it's better to know what you're getting before you make a commitment to marriage. Other couples will argue either from religious belief, the woman's fear of pregnancy, or their own personal convictions, that they'd rather wait. It isn't a question of right or wrong. It's up to the couple concerned. We older adults can best help by listening, discussing, talking the issue over with them absolutely honestly. Say what you think. A young woman has the right to say no. It's worthwhile pointing that out. She may want to say yes. As long as young people know the pros and cons, it's for them to decide, not us.

Things are, in many ways, better than they were. In an old medical book that we have at home, there's a chapter about masturbation. There's a photograph of a fine, upstanding, healthy-looking sort of chap on page 865. On page 866, there he is again, totally shot, out-of-it, like Stan Laurel with mumps. "The habits of secret vice have begun to tell on him . . . if this man escapes the asylum, he and his parents will be fortunate." At least we don't frighten the life out of young men—or women—who masturbate any more. Most young people, I hope, know that it doesn't drop off/wear out if you do; you don't go blind, barmy, or deaf. Sex is more out in the open now and that's good, but we don't want a Contraceptives-Akimbo, Do-It-At-All-Costs, Sex-As-the-Olympic-Games philosophy. Sex is much more important—and very much more complicated—than that simple approach would indicate.

"What is hell?" asks Dostoevsky. He concludes that it is the suffering that comes with being unable to love. Sex can be beautiful, exhilarating, in the context of love. So do, dear teacher—*and* parent—tell the young people about the pill, the coil and the sheath (since sexual knowledge is a human right, not a privilege), but don't forget to tell them about caring, sharing relationships. Young people and adults go wrong because they don't know how to cope with emotions—infatuation, hate, jealousy, possessiveness, fear—and with the implications of caring, really caring, about another human being. Don't forget to tell them about love.

There isn't anything dirty or horrid about sex. Me and you. Trees and flowers. How can we *sin?* Not if we really care about each other, learn to love. I once knew a woman who could only have an orgasm by having sex with men she really disliked. How sad. Sex for her was something to do with fear, with hate, with something soiled and dirty. She'd "split off". Sex was the bad part of her; her "good" side wouldn't admit that she had sexual urges, wanted nothing to do with the body. *I think; therefore, I am.* Her body was elsewhere, sullied. Descartes got it wrong. It should be I *feel,* therefore I am; we feel with our minds and our hearts and our bodies, together.

I'm no expert on sex. Who is? Those who are good at it don't talk about it. They get on with it. The only advice I can give you is to do it how you like, where you like, when you like, with someone you love (or at least like). Do it in a bin-liner, if that's your bag, and he can get in, as it were. Do it under the stars (during the summer, preferably, unless you have a tent—don't forget to take your clothes off; you ought to be past the bouncing stage by now). Express your feelings when you do it; teach him to express his emotions, talk, listen, feel, respond. That's what it's about.

Back to The Pure Drop. Hairy Tony's rabbiting on about premature ejaculation. "What d'you think about while you're doing it?" he asks me. Then he expounds, "I think about car accidents, the 101 bus route, or last Saturday's football match. It stops me from coming." Isn't it awful? I could have gone on about the beauty of sex, its deeply symbolic significance, its mystery, its vital role in communicating with another loving, caring human being. "I think about who I'm with," I said. Charlie nods. I've noticed that Old Charlie doesn't talk much about sex.

Tips towards a good sex life

○ Do your own thing. Have sex how it suits you. Have sex as frequently as it suits you (twice a day/week/year). Who's counting? It's *not* a competition. Don't believe all those stories you hear about sexual athletes. I've met one and she had the most terrible bags under her eyes.

○ *Get the sexual and romantic sides of your nature together.* Romance should be intertwined with sex. Holding hands, talking, cuddling, petting are—or can be—romantic. Make all the stops along the way. Bed should be at the end of a romantic, entrancing journey.

○ *Experiment.* You don't have to risk a strained back by attempting those funny positions in the sex manuals but do, occasionally, persuade him to take his vest off (or his hat); look at each other; try something different. Sex is one of the few remaining enjoyable pastimes that you don't need a credit card for.

○ *If you have problems—real problems—with your partner, seek advice.* The National Marriage Guidance Council offers free help with sexual problems; you'll have a local branch. The advice is confidential. Between ten and twenty percent of young married couples experience sexual difficulties. So much for the efficacy of the prevailing sex education. Sexual problems shouldn't be allowed to develop into a major marital rift.

○ *Don't exploit other people, using sex as a weapon, and don't let other people exploit you.* Good sex means equality, sharing. That's why so many men don't know the first thing about it.

○ *Be tender.* A good cuddle frequently (*very* frequently, the more the better) does you as much good, if not more, than a sexual full meal once a week. You can have both, but don't forget those cuddles (some people think they're looking for sex when what they want is warmth, closeness, touch). I think cuddling should be compulsory. That taboo-on-touch thing does an appalling amount of damage to the human heart.

○ *Tension—which springs from the Rigours of Life—is a formidable opponent of good sex.* Don't rush it. Don't forget that little things (the old-fashioned delights of courtship) mean a lot. If you're married, and have kids, get a babysitter to look after the children while you go out somewhere lonely and do it. If you live in Manchester, and there isn't anywhere lonely, do please find somebody to look after the kids for a couple of hours while you do it in the comfort of your own home. You'd cope with all the administration involved in going to your mother's/the cinema/dancing. Why not do it for sex? It's just as important, and just as enjoyable so long as you're not tensed up.

○ *Be romantic.* People may think you're a bit daft walking along holding hands, or arm in arm with your partner. Who cares? Women get depressed because they don't show anger when they feel anger; because they're prevented from loving—and being romantic—when they feel love. If you want romance, sweet tokens of affection, insist on them. It's not a lot to ask, it's free, it's a very good pathway to sex—and to mental health.

○ *Reward your partner.* Nobody can live without rewards (that's why many women quit a marriage: they never get *any*). With sex, as with everything else, praise works better than punishment or blame. Your approach should be, "That was wonderful, darling, but not in my ear. Try here. Yes, that's right." Praise people and they'll give of their best.

○ *Have fun.* It's no good if you don't have any fun—ever. Don't imitate Gertrude, but do be like Marjorie; there was a girl who knew what she wanted.

The tyranny of guilt

In the mission hall I attended as a boy, we used to sing a hymn with the refrain, "Every day'll be Sunday, by and by." *Fine,* I used to think, *but when does the talk on Africa, with lantern slides, start? That's what I'm here for.* This was my first inkling that adults spent a lot of their time living in the future. I, a child, was into living in the present—the only time we can, in fact, live in.

Those grown-ups that didn't spend time living in the future, looking forward to a day out in Brighton or Blackpool, or maybe just next Sunday, spent most of their time living in the past. "Do you remember . . . ?" That was the start of many a conversation as nostalgia cast a golden glow over times well and truly past. I could remember some of the times they were talking about, and believe me they weren't so hot—some of them were excruciatingly boring. Even now, as an adult, I've noticed that some people enjoy talking about an experience far more than they enjoy the experience itself.

You may know of that Frenchman named Proust who locked himself away and wrote eight hefty tomes entitled *A la Recherche du Temps Perdu*. Silly blighter. Those days are gone, buddy boy, all you have is the here and now. "Recalling some forgotten memory is the loss of, the regret for, a certain moment; and the houses, the roads, the avenues, have disappeared, are ghosts, like the years," writes M Proust. Of course they've gone, daft halfpenny-worth. The moving finger writes, and all that, and have you noticed the sun's shining outside? Get on with your life, while you still have time.

I'm saying all this because guilt is to do with what's gone, it's the ball and chain that past experience makes us carry around the left ankle now. The true meaning of guilt according to the *OED* is "having committed a specific or implied offence". Some of the most guilt-ridden people I know have lived fairly blameless lives, as far as I can make out, yet they go about cringing, fearful, over-polite. Stand up for yourself, for God's sake! You have as much right to be here on the earth as anybody, so stop feeling guilty about being alive, stop thinking that you've done something in the past for which you should be punished. We've all done naughty things—what's so different about you?—and if wishes were deeds, they'd have brought back hanging long ago.

The tyranny of guilt—variously called Big Mama, Mustabation or Shoulditis—imposes a crushing weight on us and stops us, in plenty of instances, from getting on with *living*. We all have obligations: things we ought to do. We all have desires: things we'd like to do. What we have to learn is to weigh up the options. What's best for me? What's best for the significant others in my life? Who gets hurt if I do this? Who gets hurt if I don't? Having weighed up the options, we choose. It's to avoid that choice—a real choice, a moral choice—that some people live out lives which are second-rate, even miserable. Human beings shouldn't waste time messing about over *there*, when they should be over *here* doing something they mean, something that they're deeply involved in. People throw their lives away because they don't like making decisions. To live in the past—or the future—absolves us from choice *and action* in the here and now.

What good is a relationship in which real feelings are never expressed? We all suffer, to some extent, from the Uriah Heep complex: we all doubt in our hearts that we really are worthy to stand upon the earth. We are. We're all born flawed (half way between beasts and angels). We win, or lose, by what we do today. We shouldn't ever make the past an excuse for not being what we'd really like to be, doing what we'd really like to do.

What if I hurt others (you ask)? Weigh up your own values and act. Nobody else can do that for you. The worst thing, in my view, is to do nothing: to be in a constant dither, a perpetual state of conflict.

Years ago, I used to work as an assistant clinical psychologist in a day hospital. We used to do a lot of group therapy: patients sitting around and telling the rest of us their stories. By and large, the patients had done nothing to feel guilty about, and yet each and every one of them was weighed down with a deep and abiding sense of guilt for something that she or he hadn't done in the first place. Blame, it seemed, had to be apportioned and they were right in there, blaming themselves.

What those people wanted was for somebody to care for them, to love them beyond reason, to cherish them. What they also needed was to forget about the unhappiness of their parents (a source of much of that guilt I've mentioned) and to get on with their own lives. There is nothing that children can do if their parents are unhappy; what *shouldn't* happen (but often does) is that the children of unhappy parents carry an enormous package of guilt with them through life. I often felt in that hospital that I should have come in one morning dressed as a judge, pointed at each patient in turn, and said, "Not guilty." They weren't guilty. They'd done nothing. Their first step towards happiness was to convince themselves that they were not to blame for what had happened to their parents.

You don't have to be a patient in a mental hospital to have problems with guilt. We all of us internalise the warnings, the cautions, the yes and no of our parents; we carry with us the standards and values of the family into which we were born. Later we may shake off some of these standards, but vestiges of the parental system remain. It's the inner voice which whispers "naughty" when we do something we feel we ought not to do.

You have to make a choice about guilt. You may want to do something, decide to do it, and feel no guilt about it whatsoever. You may decide to do something and know that you'll feel guilty about it afterwards, but be prepared to pay the price of guilt. Either way, that's fine with me—providing that you don't knowingly go out and hurt somebody. Since you can't totally escape feelings of guilt, you have to learn to handle them. The monitoring voice is inside us; we're stuck with it.

With "ordinary" people like you and me (though I'm far from ordinary, quite unique, and I know you are, too), it isn't guilt *per se* that does so much damage, because if we do something wrong, something that deeply hurts another human being, I think we *should* feel some guilt about it. What causes so much damage to human hearts and minds are those feelings of guilt which are quite disproportionate to the deed, guilt which goes on and on when the deed is long gone, guilt which prevents us from getting on with our lives, massive amounts of guilt about trivial things. We shouldn't spend our whole lives feeling guilty, doing nothing, wallowing in guilt. Life is much too important, and short, for that kind of thing.

The ways in which we punish ourselves are legion: we can marry the wrong person, provoke financial crises, make a mess of our careers. We can mix with "the wrong sort of people", take drugs, become alcoholics. If we really work at it, we can destroy ourselves. Look around you, there are lots of people who seem to provoke disasters, crises, failure—as though they want to hurt themselves.

If all else fails on the self-punishment front we can become ill—punish the body with dis-ease. There are people who enjoy operations on their body, who never stop talking about their physical ailments: life simply wouldn't be worth living if there wasn't something wrong with them—and somebody to listen to their complaints? Even the best of us, at times, revel in being hurt, gloomy, beaten. The weather's nice. "Rain's not far away," we say. With some people, rain's never very far away. They can't take too much happiness. It makes them feel uncomfortable.

Why do people try to punish themselves? The British seemingly specialise in being half-hearted, tight-lipped, wretched. There is no real need to punish yourself. Life will do it for you, sooner or later. There's no need to put your own hand to the tiller. Death gets us all in the end; if it's self-punishment, misery you're after, you must take consolation from that. The thing to do is to live until death overtakes you.

This is one thing that Cedric's on to. His philosophy—as we've noted—is Cherish the Moment, drain each day to the dregs, live all the time as though you'd just won the pools, *Live* (as the old hymn has it) *This Day as 'Twere Thy Last.* Isn't that all rather tiring (you ask)? It is. There's no wet weather programme in Cedric's life: he seems to need little rest, little time to just sit and think. Cedric's always on the go, out there, fate ever pursuing. I once asked him why. "All we have," he said, "is good moments. I want to pack in as many as possible." It's hard for me to admit this—I'm wary of Cedric's sweeping statements—but there could be some truth in it.

Where Cedric has an advantage over you and me is that his inner voice, his super-ego, doesn't seem to bother him all that much. Where you and I would be asking "Shall I?" (with the inner voice whispering, "What would mother think?"), Cedric's already in there half an hour ago, feet first. His lack of super-ego may spring from his father's comatose, almost catatonic, attitude towards life.

All Cedric's father ever did, as I saw it, was to stare at the far wall and say things like, "Is that lad at it again?" If there'd been a game called Staring At The Far Wall, Cedric's dad would have played for England. He might have been thinking about the rain, tomorrow, or yesterday. Cedric's mother was a very different kettle of fish. She used to chase Cedric the Bold, her only son, around the kitchen table shouting, "Come here, you villain." Cedric wisely refused these invitations—wisely, because his mother was usually armed with a poker (an approach recommended in few child-rearing manuals). Curiously, the effect of this kind of thing on Cedric was quite beneficial.

"My mother and father are stupid," Cedric told me when he was eight years old. He meant it. From then on he wanted very little to do with either parent's philosophy of life; he wanted to do his own thing. He was his own man, even as a child. How awful, you say. I'm not sure. It may take you thirty or forty years to get mummy off your back, rid yourself of her outlook on life (if you want or need to); it took Cedric eight. I'm not saying he was free. Nobody is. There were teachers, neighbours, bigger boys, people to stop him doing as he liked, but Cedric looked out on the world through his own spectacles. What he saw was slightly distorted, misted, but it was his very own vision.

There are several stages of moral development. At first children obey rules to avoid being punished: shouted at, smacked, frowned on. Then they conform to adult values to obtain approval: a nod, smile, or word of praise. Later they conform to authority outside of the home because there, too, he or she wishes to gain approval and avoid censure. This primitive conscience depends on other people, mostly adults, keeping an eye on children, making them feel guilty if they don't behave. Next, the child internalises the values learned and does things because, as we put it, they "ought to be done". If a child does wrong, then he or she pays the price *not* of adult disapproval (they may never find out), but of *guilt*. The moral pressure comes from inside, and so does the cost of ignoring it.

Some people can't boil an egg without worrying about it, debating whether it's right. Some people operate under doubt, hesitation, feelings of guilt—even about having a slice of bread. Mummy or daddy are always there, inside them, whispering, "Naughty." Some things are naughty, some are downright wicked. Many of the things we worry about aren't.

Take Carol. If Carol were happy, contented, even just coping, she wouldn't know what to do with herself. When it comes to self-provoked pain, Carol is top of the class. Every summer Carol falls in love with some unsuspecting oaf and adds a dash of extra-marital torment to her life. This year it's Colin. Last year it was Paul.

The scene: our garden. Enter Carol, right. She is not looking too good. To capture the right atmosphere I try to look as near as possible to Heathcliff with diarrhoea.

"Sod it," says Carol.

"You're angry, Carol," I say (psychologists say this kind of thing).

"He has this wonderful boyish grin and he works in the town clerk's department (Paul was treasury) and he's nice to talk to and . . . I love him." She looks at me defiantly. Could this be Colin she's on about?

"Does Arthur know?" I ask. Daft question. I know he doesn't know and she knows I know he doesn't know and she knows, too, like I know, that he wouldn't care too much if he did know as long as Colin didn't steal his tungsten darts. It's not Arthur that's the problem. It's Carol—or, rather, her internalised mother, the voice of conscience. "He'd kill me if he knew." I say nowt. I mean, if I say leave Arthur and go with Colin, or go back to Arthur, either way it kicks the plot into the back of a passing lorry and also means that I'm back there mowing the lawn. Besides, people have to take responsibility for themselves—even Carol.

"It's hopeless," says C. "His wife has six children and is mentally unstable. He could never leave her though his love for me is as deep as the sea." (Carol's similes, in my view, are not exactly original.) "Last Friday we had lunch together in The Boot." (I refrain from asking which make of car.) "When I'm with him I feel sixteen . . ." Throw something away, Carol, that you really like: that should do it. Given enough time, Carol will throw away Colin, especially if he's really worth knowing.

"Is there anything physical in this?" I ask. Silly question, really. All lovers do is walk towards each other on beaches. Carol looks suitably shocked.

"It's a beautiful friendship," says C. "Can't you understand that?" I can, but I'm suspicious. "There's no sex in it," says Carol. Freud believed that sex was for procreation not recreation and Carol appears to believe it, too. Last year there was no sex with Paul. Could they be putting something in the town hall tea?

"Is his wife really a mental cripple?" I ask.

"Well," says Carol, "she doesn't put his slippers out." Let's leave Carol there for the moment, on the rack. Carol likes being on racks.

It's no good saying to Carol, "You're free to do what you will; if you want it badly enough and it's against the inner voice, then you must be prepared to pay the guilt fee; it's up to you." Carol would only blame Arthur. He's the excuse for not acting.

I don't want to put Carol down, make out that she's some kind of freak. We all have these conflicts, these little battles that break out inside us. It's the way people are made. All of us have a conscience, a super-ego. We all have an id—the greedy, selfish, irrational, urgent, primitive, creative/destructive, emotional part of the personality. Sandwiched between the two is the poor little ego, self-respect, trying to keep the self-regarding sentiment in one piece, making notes as to what others think of us. We're like cooking pots on a big fire. Some of us have the lid (the super-ego) firmly on; some, like Cedric, have very loose lids, which wobble, jump up and down, or even fall off as the fire of the id warms up what's in the pot. If we take too much notice of the super-ego, we exist, hardly *live;* but if we give the id free reign, it can run away with us, destroy us.

Since Cedric lives in the present and not in the past, he is, as I've said, relatively free of guilt. "People," he's told me more than once, "get the id wrong. The id's the source of creativity." It is, at that: the id, not the ego, produced *Hamlet* and *War and Peace,* but the id also caused war, horror, torture, the death of Van Gogh, the destruction of many an artist, many an unsung heroine or hero. "The id's an untamed stallion, Cedric," I've told him. "You have to keep it safely corralled." I don't know why I bother with saying this kind of thing to Cedric, he never takes any notice of me.

While you and I spend a great deal of our lives dealing with unfinished business (mostly to do with unresolved conflicts with our own parents), Cedric seems to have had done with all that (or has he?). He certainly doesn't seem to feel guilty about the past, or to worry about the future. This gets him into some awkward scrapes, but he does get in there and lead his life. When he's done with a relationship—it usually finishes because his partner can't take his blasé attitude towards the future, his existential mode of living—he moves on to the next. He rarely suffers from emotional hang-ups; if he does, they only last for a day or two. With you and me, those emotional hang-ups (the unfinished business) can last a lifetime.

The trouble with EHUs is that they can radically affect what we do now. The mind has its own ways of evading conflict, making it less painful. It uses certain mental mechanisms to avoid the issue. *Repression* leads to instinctive energy being dammed up, and we get the person who is over-controlled, who never shows any emotion. *Sublimation* ensures that the instinctive (mainly sexual) energy is redirected. We get stamp albums, sport, aggression, spear-fishing instead of romance.

Just a minute (you say), we *can't* do what we'd like to do; we *have* to think of others. Good point, and one that Freud made himself. "Civilisation," said SF, "has been built up . . . by sacrifices in the gratification of primitive impulses . . . [The sexual forces] are in this way sublimated, that is to say, their energy is turned aside from its sexual goal and diverted towards other ends, no longer sexual and socially more valuable." Freud regarded the control of sexual impulses as essential to more culturally oriented achievements.

Civilised men and women, to deal with their more primitive urges, use *fantasy* (think about it but don't do it) and *rationalisation*

(I should have done it but it was Tuesday—a bad day for me—and, besides, I had the tea/Arthur/my new hair-do to think about). They use *intellectualisation* (talking about it, discussing it, never getting around to doing it) and *projection* (it's those others that have all those nasty, sexual thoughts and impulses, not me). Animals eat each other; human beings—part animals, part angels—sometimes beat each other (mostly, they just eat each other psychologically). It is a rather deviant, cowardly way of keeping one's self-esteem.

Maurice uses *regression*—reverting back to more savage modes of behaviour—to cope with his frustrations (we all do it). If Jenny, in his mind, is his mum and he, in his mind, is a child who has been frustrated, you can imagine the result will be far from edifying. Sometimes this situation can lead to violence; it can lead to verbal insults which would shock a brewer's drayman; it can, as we know, lead to murder.

When human beings abandon their rational minds, give full reign to their unconscious impulses, all hell can break loose. That's why I'm *not* saying to imitate Cedric and do everything. I'm only saying, the choice is yours, and your rule must be that you hurt nobody or, at a pinch, as few people as is possible. You and your poor old ego are Piggy in the Middle. The super-ego is a necessary defence; especially when you consider the power of the id.

By now, you'll be feeling low. What the hell (you may well inquire) is the solution to all these tricks of the mind, these powerful unconscious impulses? The answer is, *you must become more aware of the unconscious impulses inside you* and don't be afraid to deal with them—only you can decide how. *Finish your unfinished emotional business and grow up;* insist on other people treating you as an adult and have nothing to do with them if they start to use you as an emotional punch-bag. *Say what you want from a relationship;* this gives people little chance to foist their less salubrious fantasies onto you, giving you the paper bag of their emotional hang-ups to carry around. *Come off the guilt bit.* The past is over and done. Live in the present—think for yourself, make up your own mind, be aware of the justifiable, more reasonable, more acceptable needs of others—but don't feel guilty about yourself. I would only blame you if you never did anything; that, to me, seems a waste of precious time.

We *should* feel guilty that children in Uganda, Cambodia, and India starve to death, that the expectation of life in parts of Africa is less than forty years, that roughly forty percent of the world's population is still illiterate, that millions of human beings in the great family of man are born to hunger. Organisations like Oxfam do what they can to help. What do you do, as an individual? It's a luxury to feel guilty about personal problems in the face of the vast amount of suffering which takes place in underprivileged countries.

Nearer home, we have our own poor: our homeless, our unemployed, the physically handicapped—the blind, the deaf, the damaged, the immobile. We have mentally handicapped children and adults, children with incurable diseases, people injured in road accidents. We have tramps, human derelicts, alcoholics, the chronically depressed, the old and infirm. In The Pure Drop, some pretty woman says to me, "I'm having an affair with Quintin. He's married. I feel terribly guilty about it." I feel very sad. I feel like saying, "It's Quintin's choice, and yours. Think about it and, if you're desperate, get on with it." However, while she's messing about—indulging in guilty feelings, wandering about the litter-strewn shore of her mind—she should also think about that vast ocean of suffering that's out there. "Do your thing with Quintin, do, then spare a thought for men and women who have nothing but suffering. There's enough pain about without you inventing it."

"Game of ping-pong?" a thalidomide boy used to greet me at his special school. His hands stuck out of his shoulders; he had no arms. "You're too good for me," I'd say; I couldn't see the joke, but he could. Another boy I used to see was suffering from muscular dystrophy; in those days they died in their mid-teens. When he reached the falling-over stage, he still insisted on playing football with me. "Watch this," he'd say, as he'd run at the ball and fall over. You could see his calves getting larger as the degeneration of his muscles progressed. From his wheelchair, he'd say to me, "Arsenal are thinking of giving me a trial." I didn't like that kind of humour; it tended to make me want to cry. "What's heaven like?" he asked me in the hospital. "Free fish and chips," I told him. He smiled. "Don't think I'll make it for the Arsenal now." I held his hand, then I went. He died on the Saturday. I hope I was right about the fish and chips: I liked that boy a lot.

I'm not telling you this to make you feel guilty—unless you're feeling guilty about wasting time feeling guilty. I *would* dearly wish you to get your own problems into perspective and to apportion blame where blame is truly due. I remember someone once said to me, "My mother's ruined my life." She hasn't. You must accept responsibility for yourself. If *your* life is ruined, you must blame yourself, not her or anybody else. I've seen mothers that would make Jaws seem quite friendly. What's so specially awful about yours? If you can't grow up—say "I'm me" *and* "I'm responsible for me"—then you're condemned to live in the past and be miserable, but let's get it straight: you were the judge, you did the sentencing, and you sent yourself down for life. Other people would give anything to have a chance to live.

Have nothing to do with guilt. It's a useless, stupid, destructive emotion. It's self-indulgence, self-pity of the very worst sort. Reflect, think about it, then do what you think is right. Stick up for yourself. Care about your life. Respect yourself and respect others. Who needs guilt instead of a valid self-regarding sentiment? If you must feel guilty, save it for those around you who have little or nothing. There are plenty of people who deserve our sorrow, even shame, rather than wasting that kind of emotion on ourselves.

Pointers towards emancipation from guilt

○ *Having nothing to do with guilt feelings.* Those guilt zones within the hidden recesses of your personality do nothing for you, or for the rest of us, for that matter.

○ *Live in the here and now, as much as possible.* Whether we like it or not, time that's past *is* past. Have no—or few—regrets. What's done is done, water under the bridge. Why waste energy on all that?

○ *Feel good about yourself.* Feeling bad is an indulgence: self-pity. I doubt whether you're in the rape, pillage and loot category, so don't be too hard on yourself. You've only one life, so make the most of it.

○ *Don't blame others.* Carol never did make it with Colin; she said Arthur put the psychological boot in. I had a feeling it would all come to dust. It was nothing to do with Arthur, though. Carol's great but she has guilt feelings about eating an apple. I hope you're a little more daring than that.

○ *Don't waste time and energy.* Guilt feelings squander both. You have only a limited amount of either, so why fritter them away on the useless pastime of feeling guilty?

○ *Don't over-control your world.* Do a few zany things occasionally, leave yourself open to some good experiences. If you don't enter the game, you don't lose, but that seems to me a very cowardly and defeatist—even miserable—attitude towards life.

○ *Don't mess up the lives of others with your own leftover guilt.* Be an adult; ask others to treat you as an adult. Never wallow in guilt; it doesn't do your loved ones—significant others—any good at all.

○ *Get your value system straight.* What do you really believe in? Weigh up your actions, *act:* take responsibility for yourself. You can hardly expect somebody else to come along and do the job for you. Why should somebody else play parent to you?

○ *Don't let others manipulate you by making you feel worthless or guilty.* You're worth a lot. Make sure you put that point across. Don't let yourself be abused and then start feeling sorry for yourself.

○ *You're after respect, fun, happiness.* It's your right to seek them, to handle the bouquets and brickbats that accompany the search. Avoid people who pity you, or would like to. Who needs pity? Life's too short for that.

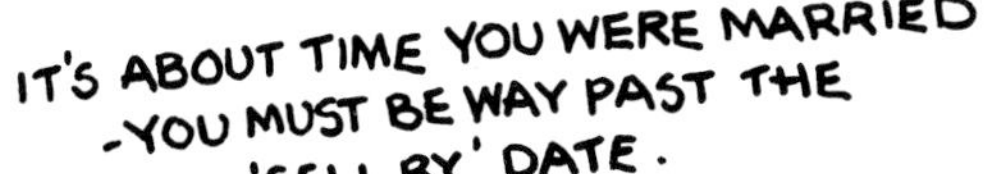

Map out your marriage

My friend Geoff once filled me in on the significance of the nuptial scenario. "In a society starved of ritual, of ceremony," quoth he, "a wedding is one of the few remaining universally accepted Rites of Passage. It's a dramatic act in which two people come together to re-define their lives. It is an initiation ceremony in which these two individuals promise, henceforth, to construe their lives as a couple." Phew. Many sociologists talk thus. "It is usually," I told *him*, "also a rare chance to get some free booze."

Of course, you can swear to be true to each other in a car park, or on the back seat of a No 73 bus. A friend of mine was "married" on a hillside overlooking the sea. His best friend read out a passage from Keats; afterwards, we all swam in the waves, the women's flowered dresses billowing out like sea anenomes in the water. Then we drank wine and danced into the early hours by a campfire. "Wha's goin' on, then?" a passing yokel asked me. "A wedding," I told him. "Thaa's a funny sort of weddin'," said he, staring at two of the women who'd brought bathing costumes and bathrobes.

The snag with this kind of ceremony is that you don't get a licence, nor the approval of the State or Church (or of your Aunt Maud). It could be the *feeling* of being "properly" (ie, legally) wed that makes many young brides prefer a register office to car park or bus, and even more to opt for a church to avoid the railway waiting room atmosphere of your average RO. Symbolism and ritual are deeply comforting to us. Who can deny that a church wedding is a beautiful way to start a new life?

Anyway, let's start with Jenny. She had the lot: white wedding gown, penguin suits for the men, Bridal March on the church organ, hymns, bells, limousines, and confetti. Despite the groom's side of the aisle being filled with what appeared to be a collection of gangsters and their molls, it was a lovely wedding.

"Wilt thou serve him, love, honour, and keep him in sickness and in health, and, forsaking all others, keep thee only unto him?" Beautiful words, but be careful, Jenny. You're twenty-five now. Staying faithful to one man for what could be fifty years is a pretty tall order. "*Que será, será,*" I remark to my wife, only to be kicked on the shin by my daughter for whispering. When you're married, you don't do what you like.

I've no doubt that Jenny and Maurice were taking it seriously. I'm sure that neither of them was there to see me looking tidy, for once, or to shake hands with near and distant relatives ancient and modern, or to enjoy the cold salad tuck-in provided by the bride's father. They were there taking it seriously, making an important commitment, as most of us do when we get married.

Let's have a few facts about marriage. Marriage, like rheumatism, gets most of us in the end. Ninety-five percent of women, ninety-one percent of men have been married by the age of forty. Most of us seem to agree that marriage itself is A Good Thing. It's making the whole thing work that appears to be getting harder.

Divorce has increased threefold since ten years ago. If this current trend of more divorces persists, it is probable that one in four marriages that took place during the 'Seventies will have ended in divorce before the twenty-fifth anniversary; fewer and fewer of us will be celebrating our Silver Wedding anniversaries.

There is an inverse relationship between age at marriage and risk of divorce. Roughly twice as many teenagers get divorced as people marrying in their late twenties. A high proportion of teenage marriages, more than a quarter, break down before the "Tin

Wedding" (ten years). Not surprising, since young people are still growing emotionally, and it's hard to wake up in the morning to find that you've married a stranger. Then, too, teenagers are likely to be surrounded by people who are still unmarried (lack of moral support) or are likely to have married because of pregnancy and with little money behind them—not the best of starts to what is, after all, a somewhat fraught enterprise.

Even us golden oldies (this year I shall have been twenty-two years before the mast) can't say with any certainty that we'll be in there celebrating our Gold or Diamond Wedding, even if we live that long. The good ship *Marriage* is sailing over stormy seas, and glimpses of those tranquil, sunlit shores we all expected to reach are becoming rarer, it seems. Our friends appear to be falling, nuptial-wise, like leaves in autumn.

I think that if there were a viable alternative to marriage, we would have found it by now. Communes, by and large, don't work. They don't provide sufficient security and privacy. Not many people have the courage to face life single-handed: with freedom comes loneliness, and a self-centredness which, sometimes, eats away at the human soul. Living together *is* becoming increasingly popular, but usually as a prelude to, rather than a substitute for, the "till death us do part" promise.

Taking into account the risks, the sheer hard work involved, why is marriage still so popular? The Good News is that marriage provides us with continuity, a history, as well as a safe (sometimes) base from which we may spring out to tackle a largely hostile or indifferent world. It's surprising, when you ask women what's good about marriage they mostly tell you the same thing (well, the dozen I queried did, put it that way).

Marriage can provide you with children, more money (single parents are mostly poorer than the rest of us), and *sharing*. Hopefully it gives you somebody who remains constant, and *for* you when others are against you; regular cuddles (just as important to the women I asked as regular sex); sharing the good and the bad, emotional support, the pleasures of *companionship*.

The sharing and companionship bits are, in my view, crucial. When distance and non-communication creep into a marriage, it's heading for the rocks. It's empathy and closeness that are vital, not sex (anyway, good sex *implies* sympathy and closeness). Those women I know who have folded their tents and gone elsewhere weren't looking for sex. "I couldn't talk to him any more. We had nothing in common." *That* (ie, loss of friendship) is what kills most marriages—and not too astonishing either.

One amazing truth emerges on the positive side. *The great majority of couples who get married stay together till one of them dies.* They stick to that "death us do part" promise. This magnificently irrational behaviour—considering all the stresses and strains—says something about the deep need of people to *create* something, and to have a lasting commitment to something which is more important than themselves. Despite all the different social attitudes to marriage, despite changes in the divorce law, people still stagger on through snow and ice under that banner with the strange device: *Married.* They can't all be deluded. There must be something in it.

Before I get too sentimental, let's have a look at the dark side. A cynical Frenchman once said that a woman waits for the right man to come along, and in the meantime she gets married. Marriage is the cure for love, claims Cedric. George Bernard Shaw wrote, "Marriage is tolerable enough in its way, if you're easy-going and don't expect too much from it. But it doesn't bear thinking about."

What's grotty about marriage? Everybody I questioned said, "Lack of freedom." Yet, I ask, isn't human freedom choosing the most comfortable prison?.

To the gist. Most of the marriages I know are far from the textbook-happy, close unions that people dream about when they tie the knot. They are fairly rickety, loosely tied parcels of humanity held together by patience, love, and a determination to succeed. Marriage is best when it's fuelled on love. It's no good without some appreciation, some reward: everybody needs stroking. Few of us can survive in an emotional wilderness, just doing the day's work (there's plenty of that) and getting nothing in return. In the beginning was the word and the word was *sharing.*

Let's get back to Jenny and Maurice. Once married, they, like the rest of us, re-defined their lives. They discussed mutual friends over breakfast and supper. Arthur, a great pal of the groom's before the wedding day, had to go. Jenny positively loathed the local piss-artist, Arthur, and swiftly put the boot in on Thursday Night Out With The Lads. Maurice, who had seen these evenings as a source of good companionship, innocent merriment, and great *fun,* was speedily disabused of the notion. He began to see them for what they were (or as Jenny saw them): a threat to the sobriety of their union and a needless drain on the joint bank account.

More facts. There is a high incidence of divorce during the first four years of marriage (when we're trying to adjust to each other) and another peak among people who have been married for more than twenty years (this is when the children have departed and married people have to face up to each other *as a couple* for the first time in many years). Jenny and Maurice got through the first four years all right. Crisis time, for them, came later.

I don't wish to be unfair, but, in the initial stages of marriage, Jenny wrote most of the script. She bore two children and played the part of the Good Mother in the little play that was enacted. She sprang forth with the Elastoplast and fish fingers where necessary. She talked to the children, attended to their bodily and emotional requirements. Meanwhile, off centre stage, Maurice got on with his career in the Lifelong Accident and Insurance Company. Whether the arrangement was fair or not, nobody questioned. It was a clear job demarcation, with Jenny getting most of the hard toil and dirty work. She didn't complain. She just accepted that that is what mothers of young children do.

The crunch, Crisis Time, came when Jenny took the second child to the gates of the infant school and left him in the charge of that establishment's noise abatement officers. "How long do I have to stay here?" asked the boy, as Jenny walked off down the road. "Two years," Jenny shouted back at him. "Don't forget to collect me," came a faint voice from the playground.

Jenny bought herself a second-hand Citroën that symbolised, for her, independence. She could go where she liked and nobody could track her down. She got herself a part-time job at the local hospital and even, wicked woman, bought herself some new clothes out of her own earnings, *and* (this gets worse) insisted upon putting her money into a separate bank account, to give her a feeling of independence, of being a person in her own right—as opposed, or in addition to, the back-breaking role of the Good Mother. Then she joined the Open University and went off to summer school, *by herself*. Goodness me.

This, dear reader, wasn't Act II, Scene I. It was a whole new production, as though, after the interval, the play had changed from *Mother Courage* to a Busby Berkeley spectacular. Maurice found it hard to understand. I distinctly heard him whisper "Traitor" as we all waved Jenny off. He waved a grubby tea-towel and that was really his last sign of animation.

Three times during the ensuing week I found him at the top of the stairs, head in his hands. Once he was actually crying in his kitchen. "What's the matter?" I asked him, but he didn't have to tell me. Tarzan—him good swing through trees of Lifelong Assurance—no good cook beans, talk to children. The Me-Tarzan/You-Jane pantomime had had the curtain well and truly rung down on it by Jenny's insistence on individuality.

Maurice took it hard, as well he might: he'd had no rehearsal for this new script and some of the scenes he envisaged over the dishes and frying pan were, to say the least, beyond the pale. Jenny could take a lover; there was no way of keeping up with her movements now she was mobile. She might discover that he, Maurice, wasn't the greatest thing between the sheets since Valentino and where did that leave him? Maurice was a worried man.

This is one of those make-or-break stages in marriage. The wife shakes off her symbiotic ties to husband and children and starts to blossom out as a person. Don't underestimate Maurice. Emotionally dyslexic, like most men, and with his own mother and father's marriage based on the palaeolithic model, he had little in the way of a Good Marriage Guide. He was, I might add, no more chauvinistic than most men. No matter. Maurice *was* distraught. "I've given her two beautiful children," he told me (surely she had a hand in that, too?). "I've always provided her with plenty of money" (yes, but is the concept of dad as money-box entirely satisfactory?). "Why this, then?" he queried. Hard to say, except to suggest that perhaps Jenny had plans of her own, was beginning to see the world through her own perceptual spectacles rather than through his.

Over the next six months he changed. He adapted. He started (this is true) to tidy up around the house, bring wife and kids cups of tea in bed, and even vacuum the living room. He bought a paperback cookery book and tried his hand at risotto and other dishes. I saw him kissing Jenny in the garden. "A woman likes to be kissed behind the rhododendrons," I told Maurice. He'd become openly affectionate towards her; it was as though, somehow, he was scared of losing her. What a pity, I thought (I've always had this philosophical outlook), that Jenny hadn't gone away for a week during the first years of marriage. Even if it were only to her mother's, it would have been well worth it just to give Maurice some insight into what being with two young children all day is really like.

M suffered from withdrawal symptoms (ie, withdrawal from that paternal paradise which he'd lost, or been hurled from) for quite some time. During that first year (AD1—After Dismantling), I crept up to him in the garden while he was having a little doze. "Open University," I whispered in his ear. "Gerroff," he shouted, jumping up and waving his arms. Men and women, I thought, are strangers. They work together, live together, sleep together, but oft a gap, a psychic rift remains. Why? For a start, we have two thousand years (at least) of misunderstandings to make up for. I'm sure we'll get it together sometime. Or some of us will.

Maurice did, as much as anyone does. After ten years of marriage, he was forced to try to get to know the woman he lived with. He gave up being John Wayne, or Tarzan, Our Hero. He started, in ever such a modest kind of way, to be himself. It was a step in the right direction, and it seemed to save the day . . .

Although their problems aren't over yet (are they ever? there I go again, being philosophical), let's leave J and M for the time being and turn to the question of why some couples split up and why others stay together. This is a great mystery. Even Sherlock Holmes would have been puzzled as to why Simon and Pauline (both

Beautiful People and, on the face of it, a marriage of twin souls, made in heaven) should separate after two years, while the Utterly Lovely Liz and Super-Grot Cyril, the one who sniffs all the time and has a cough like a seal in agony, are still together after fifteen.

One thing's for sure: this paradox has nothing at all to do with legality. The Divorce Law Reform Act came into effect in 1971 and the consolidating Matrimonial Causes Act says that the sole cause for divorce is that the marriage has "irretrievably broken down". Fine, but what does *broken down* mean? What's *irretrievably*?

A woman complained to me that her husband, a window cleaner, kept coming home in the day to make love to her. I inquired (I have this prurient turn of mind, too) about frequency. "Five or six times," she said. She thought this was odd and wondered if he were a sex maniac. I asked myself if we shouldn't have *Multi-Coloured Swap Shop* (for husbands) on television. I know some women who'd be glad of a man like that, and they don't even have dirty windows.

No judge can legislate for human folly. Proof of irretrievable breakdown? One clause is, "The respondent has behaved in such a way that the petitioner cannot reasonably be expected to live with him or her." On this basis I'm surprised that Liz lasted five minutes, never mind fifteen years. Cyril, besides cleaning out both his ears with his right index finger at meals (not easy to do), gives his guests whisky in wine glasses: a good reason for divorce, to my mind, considering that they have tumblers in the cupboard. Cedric snores like an elephant in labour and yet Barbara, his wife, stayed with him for all of ten years. Any other woman would have moved houses—or emigrated, to be on the safe side—in the first week.

Sometimes folly or insanity or a liking for quarrels holds marriages together. I'm not saying that these darker-side-of-the-moon marriages should be used as models—only that it's very curious what does hold people together.

We all have examples of the Strange Marriage bit and not, by any means, all psychiatric cases. There's Beryl, married to George, nine stone. Do they use rope and tackle or is George, like that cereal, shot from a gun? I know couples who never eat together (as the Duchess of Windsor said of the Duke, "I married him for better or worse, but not for lunch"), never sleep together, never discuss anything together. I know a couple who have sex once every six weeks; that seems awfully sparse to me but they seem to be perfectly contented with the score card. There's Arnold, a sailor, and Bill, North Sea rigs, who are away for most of the year: their wives don't complain. "It's great when we're together," they tell me. Most odd. Togetherness, it seems, doesn't mean being together all the time.

I know a couple who are into a game called the Battle of the Somme. They argue, but they don't have the sort of arguments that you have. This is the real thing. Shoot-out stuff. She's stabbed him twice (once with a carving knife, once with a chisel), broken a very large mirror over his head, hit him with an electric hostess trolley. This is an impressive witness to the power hidden within some smaller women. He's been to hospital so often that they call him by his first name up in casualty.

He's no saint, either. Her silhouette is there, all over the walls, where he's thrown cups of coffee at her. Each shape records, presumably, a direct hit. The house reminds me of pictures I've seen of Hiroshima. The ironing board, armchair, and sewing machine he's also thrown (he could be on health foods) have left chips in the woodwork. "Does it all happen slowly?" I've asked them. "Like in Sam Peckinpah?" They can't remember. "More rapid than slow," he says. Time goes quickly when you're happy. "It doesn't alter our relationship," she tells me, guardedly.

The games are innumerable. Men like to play *Little Boy Lost* (needs a cub mistress or a nanny, not a wife, a partner); *Malayan Tea Planter* (you brown girl, smile shyly, bring tiffin); *This Sporting Life* (enters your soirée wearing rubber flippers and snorkel or waving a squash racquet—you may begin to wonder if you marry this type whether your role is merely to stand on the touchline and field his balls); *Popeye* (the macho type with big biceps who needs a really dumb woman to admire him—tell this man that God went to Mount Olive and he'll think you're being blasphemous); *Hide-and-Seek* (he hides in the pub, in the shed, next door—anywhere there's no responsibility involved—and you have to look for him).

Of course, you don't have to play these games if you don't want to. It's rather like watching television. Most of it is the most appalling rubbish, but if the worst comes to the worst you can always switch off. Men, since it's men we're talking about, have to be taught *in the early stages of marriage* that if they play daft immature games, they play alone.

The worst game of all is *Masters and Servants* (sometimes called *Foxes and Rabbits*, where one eats and the other is eaten, psychologically speaking). What happens here is that one partner cruises around the highways and byways of life, while the other acts as a human garage, tanking him up, servicing him, supplying various spare parts when required. Some men—the type known as the Narcolept—go no further than the armchair, but they still require servicing. In return, they sleep and eat. There is very little return on the vast energy that the active partner puts into the relationship.

Not all men are into relationships. "An ideal wife," a regular at The Pure Drop told me, "would be a good-looking waitress without knickers." This is called, in some quarters, the Deaf and Dumb Nymphomaniac Syndrome. This yearning for a blow-up partner is prevalent among men who, sadly, have never learned to look upon women as real people. You can gather that any notion of *sharing* with this kind of man is doomed to disappointment.

To look at the patterns of marriage is like looking down a kaleidoscope being held by a drunken man. Even when people aren't being pathological and deliberately destroying themselves, or playing games (which are, quite frequently, unconsciously chosen), there are still the most unexpected unions.

Take the case of my wife and myself. My wife was hoping for a practical man: shelves, bookcases, mending fuses, that kind of thing. She ought to have known. Years ago, before we were married, we camped (but no sex; this was before it was invented) at night on a traffic roundabout. "Good spot, this," I said. "Quiet." When we woke up we were surrounded by cars. "No man is an island," I said, never lost for the aphorism. That's not the point, though.

The night before, she'd been expecting me to erect the bivouac. "You did National Service," she said. Listen, sweetheart (through the teeth), I had a batman to do that kind of thing for me, carry my revolver, all the heavy things. I spent most of the time walking around Kenya saying "Good morning" to the Mau Mau. Neither my wife nor I got what we wanted, or expected. Mind you, I still like her. I think she still likes me despite the fact that both of us have, many times, behaved in such a way that neither of us could be *reasonably* expected to live with each other. I'm not sure that marriage is, in the last analysis, anything to do with reason.

It's all a bit of a mystery, especially what makes couples split up. A friend, a real old pal, had been married twelve years. She'd been fairly happy, had an average amount of good and bad times. He was, and is, intelligent, good-looking, slightly vain but not unkind. One Thursday evening she cleaned her teeth, put a few things in a bag, walked out, went back ("I'd forgotten my moisturising cream," she told me, with horror) and, before she did her Captain Oates, addressed a few words to her spouse. "I'm going," she said. "Your dinner's in the oven. I won't be back." Nor was she. Tremendous courage, considering that she had nowhere to go.

"Why?" I asked her.

"I didn't like the way he asked me for a clean shirt when he came in," she said. It isn't, of course, the real reason. They'd been drifting apart, as friends, as people who spoke to each other, did things with each other, for years. The shirt incident sparked off her yearning to be treated as a real person, ignited her drastic act.

What's interesting about this departure was the reaction of her two children, one boy, one girl. "You won't forget my new shoes?" asked the lad. "Can I still go on having piano lessons?" asked her daughter. So much for generalisations about the effect of separation on children. Children *don't* like parents to divorce, but they can sometimes understand it when they do and they can remain friends with both parents if they're not used, and abused, in the quarrel between the adults. "Are you missing me at home?" my friend asked her two children. "No," they replied, "but Spot is, terribly." It's nice to know somebody cares, even if it's only the dog.

It's little things that act as a focus for long-standing feelings of alienation, distance. "Salt," a husband of another friend of mine used to say to her. No "please". She left him last year and hasn't been back. It wasn't politeness, or sex, she was seeking. "I suddenly realised that I didn't like him," she told me, "so what was the point? We simply had nothing in common." I'm a romantic about staying together, seeing it out, but I'm realistic enough to see that with some couples there *is* no point. The truth for them is that, whichever way you look at it, they are simply not going to fulfil their potential as individuals, make it as people, if they stay together. Better to part, and continue to grow, than to remain partners and damage each other irretrievably.

To be honest, marriages that break up seem no worse—from the outside—than those that don't. I suspect it's growing older, being aware of lost chances, the passing of time, that's part of the pain. Sometimes we seek a one-last-chance at youth, love, and ecstasy outside the rigorous confines of marriage. Once out, we find that every situation has boundaries, limits, drawbacks, elements of reality, and that our dreams of love and ever-lasting youth are just as vulnerable with Julian or Fred or Imogen or Meg as they are with whomever it is you're espoused to. The grass in the next field is always greener—until we get there. Escape isn't always the answer.

Let's face it, modern couples do make tremendous demands upon each other emotionally, practically, conversationally. Is it possible to love the same person for fifty years? Not romantically, perhaps, but in other ways. Is it possible to have something to say to each other all that time? Sometimes, in a restaurant, with my wife in an I'll-be-glad-if-you'll-be-frank mood, I wonder. In the old days of the extended family, I doubt whether couples saw so much of each other. My mother and father, because of his work, only really met each other on Saturday night and Sunday. I should imagine (though I've no proof) that they only made love on a Sunday afternoon when we kids were at Sunday school, and they were alone and not tired.

Couples today are with each other much more. That makes for companionship—providing that you enjoy one another's company. It also means that you get to know each other eventually. That can be very pleasant. It can also be a shock, or even the end of the union.

My mother and father's marriage was static. They weren't going anywhere. They stayed in the same place all their lives, didn't change much as people, carried out their appointed tasks from Day One until my father died. He worked, she took care of home and family; he stayed in the same job all his life, she stayed by her post at the oven and kitchen sink. It started off not as *Love on the Dole*, but love on £3 10s per week; although his wages went up, nothing changed very much. Their friends remained the same. Why shouldn't they? They always went to the same places, met the same people, had a weekly routine. Their life was horizontal, not vertical. They had no ambitions. They had what they wanted and were content.

Modern marriage isn't like that. It's shifting, moving, evolving. Many young couples see their progress as vertical: going up. Roles have to change as the marriage evolves and circumstances alter. Marriages grow, alter direction and aim. The relationship you have with your husband when the children are infants is not the same as the relationship you have when the children are older, as Maurice will confirm. It cannot be: a woman who is released from the all-encompassing, gut-snapping demands of bringing up babies and youngsters is going to define herself afresh when she grasps her newly found freedom. The new freedom can lead to growth within a marriage, or to the end of it. We have to work out ways of giving *privacy, space to grow* to each partner if we want to stay the course.

Most of the marriages I know are, to be frank, rather like those serials they used to show at children's matinées in the old days—with people tied to railway lines, hanging from cliffs, being pursued by a crocodile, jaws open. You always had to wait until next week to see what happened. Few marriages I know are like *The Sound of Music*. My own marriage based its early years on the MCP model. I started off as Hopalong Cassidy (Butch Cassidy, for younger readers), giving orders in a Western drawl, slouching about the place, a Hero. My wife was Mother Hubbard, and glad of the part. Since then, we've been through *The Fred Astaire Show* (me in the dancing shoes) and *The Tall Man Rides Out* (me as Clint Eastwood). Slowly, it changed. I suddenly found I was playing in a show called *A Woman of Real Importance*, me with a walk-on part. My own roles got smaller and smaller, the kids and my wife started running the town. I settled for the part of the surly bartender, and the kids and missus became the steely-eyed ones. What's that? Orange juice with ice and three straws. Comin' up, Lulu. Actually for the last few years we've scrapped these plays, stopped acting. I, for one, have decided to be myself and get to know the others.

On the face of it, marriage these days shouldn't work. As well as the bizarre scenarios, the play-acting, the games, there are plenty of other factors militating against happiness and longevity. There are the practical demands, the hard work, the lack of privacy, the money troubles (just look at the price of houses for young couples and the cost of existing, never mind living), the frustrations, the pain, those daily tasks that offer little spiritual reward and that—without other rewards—slowly grind you down. Yet, strangely enough, marriage has never been so popular. More people than ever get married—and, sadly, divorced. The vast majority of people who divorce wish to remarry. Why? What, in view of this chapter of accidents, is so attractive about this institution called marriage?

Marriage can be a bastion, a stronghold, a retreat, a safe base in a world which is becoming increasingly confusing and unsafe. Marriage, for many of us, *has* to work. We have simply nothing else left to believe in. We need a partner, a pal. Closeness is crucial, and if you don't get it from your spouse, where do you get it? Lack of empathy breaks up many marriages. Sharing (fun, sadness, tears) holds many more together, so does the dread of loneliness, the fear of the chill out there beyond the family hearth.

I think we all expect too much—from marriage, and from "society", ie, ourselves. In marriage, a man expects a good cook, a charming hostess, a whore in bed. A woman expects a DIY expert, a delightful companion, a good conversationalist, a demon lover. Rarely are all these talents combined within the one human frame. If your husband looks like Paul Newman, it is unlikely that he will be a brilliant decorator and come forth with a ceaseless flow of epigrams, like a latter-day Oscar Wilde or Noel Coward. I always say I'd like to have married a woman who could mend broken slates on the roof, wittily, and look sexy at the same time. It's a lot to expect.

Marriage can provide us with companionship, a chance to grow through responsibility, hard work, and trust. It can't provide everlasting romance and happiness. It *can* provide us with a framework within which to work at our lives; there will be setbacks and quarrels, but hopefully these will fuel our journey towards maturity rather than holding us back. I once met a cleaning lady in a school who told me that she'd been married for forty years and never had an argument with her husband. What kind of relationship was that? If you live with someone, surely you must expect, if you are both real people with needs of your own, to disagree sometimes?

We have assumed that progress in this modern world inevitably means more of everything: more food, more roads, more cars, more fridge/freezers, more dishwashers, more divorce, more sex, and more women's liberation. I doubt that we have the material resources on this planet to produce, and run, millions more cars. And every car produced adds to the pollution of our environment. I doubt whether we have the social resources to cope with an ever-increasing divorce rate; we may get better at learning to stay married, supporting each other and those couples at risk who surround us. These increasing demands cannot be met.

It's *quality* I'd like to see more emphasis on, not quantity. Not more sex, but better sex. Not more women's liberation, but a move to give women the justice and equality and opportunities to which they are entitled as citizens and human beings. Sisters, don't ask for more, never ask for freedom (that's another myth), just ask for what you're entitled to, and insist upon it. Don't scream to be like men (look around you at the disastrous males making a mess of their lives), just keep saying, quietly and firmly, that you want your rights as people so that you, too, may have a chance to live life more abundantly, more richly.

Is it possible that we are on the way to seeing *less* of the things that we have taken for granted? We may be ready to plateau off, with cars, fridge/freezers—and divorce. We may (who knows?) return to some old values, different ways of looking at things. Maybe loyalty will make a comeback, seeing it out, working at it, instead of expecting the world (or our spouse) to owe us a living. As my old granny used to say, "You can expect things to work, and to be worthwhile, only if you work at them." Maybe we'll lower our unreal expectations, shift them in the direction of *quality*. Maybe we'll all become less selfish and think about others just for a change.

I could be wrong. Perhaps the divorce rate *will* reach one in three marriages, people will experiment with communes again, or more and more couples will live together but not get married. I doubt it, personally. As we think more closely about society and how to survive, I think we'll realise that the *only* way to survive is to re-establish the Big Four: Love, Loyalty, Community Feeling, and Forgetting Oneself For Five Minutes. We just have to learn, after two decades of selfishness, to live together in friendship, that's all.

We've been a little romantic about what to expect, what it's all about. The reality is that you and I grow old, we won't always wear sloganed T-shirts and the bottom of our Levi jeans rolled up. Our hair will grey, and we'll slowly but surely lose our figures and young looks. It's already happened to me. We will come across pain, and poverty, and malice, and murder, and spite, and the threat of nuclear disaster. We'll live in the future, as we live now, in danger, in insecurity. We need something to believe in, and one of the things we'll come to believe in is unselfishness, thinking about others. It'll dawn on us all, sooner or later, that no man (or woman, either) is an island, as I keep saying. We win, or lose, together.

That's where old-fashioned marriage may make its reappearance. For the young people I talk to, it may have already done so. They *mean* those promises. The whole enterprise means a great deal to them. "Wilt thou comfort her, honour and keep her in sickness and in health, and forsaking all others, keep thee only to her, so long as ye both shall live?" Who in their right minds would do such a thing?

Plenty of people I know would. Lots of those youngsters, for a start. "I've had a good time before marriage, I admit that," one twenty-three-year-old told me. "When I marry this year, it's for good. That's terribly important to me. I really believe in the 'till death do us part' thing. Silly, isn't it?" Not really. Can you think of something better?

I saw an old couple at the seaside, on Weymouth promenade, sitting on one of those green benches. The pair of them must have been near eighty. Both were fast asleep, she with her head on his chest, her white hair falling down onto his pullover. I wondered why they'd stayed together all those years. Crazy, really. Perhaps, if I'd woken them up to ask them, they'd have said, "It's just the idea, you see." I imagined them at home, sitting at each end of the sofa, like bookends, watching television. I noticed their wrinkled hands.

Perhaps (there's a thought) they weren't married to each other. Maybe this was a lover's tryst, a brief afternoon together away from their spouses, and the excitement of it all had tired them out. Maybe they were married, their fourth time around. Isn't life complicated?

Where marriage doesn't work, people are often very keen to get married again, give it a second try. That doesn't surprise me. People need an ideal, an idea, a goal, something to work for, especially when it's something outside of, more important than, themselves. To live, most of us need more than a Habitat-furnished room, some Elkie Brooks LPs, a washbasin and a mirror. We need to create something, one way or another, that lasts. That's the big one.

You may have kids; they can extinguish the flames of love faster than anything I know. It's hard to sit—or lie—there loving each other if your eldest wants his rugby jersey washed that minute or if the Whine of the Week is holding a dripping lolly over your face. There's nothing like the presence of children to extinguish the flames of passion, instantly. Two's company. Two and two halves can complicate matters.

To cope in today's world you need to keep reassessing the role of everybody in the family. You really must keep on adapting to new situations, new dynamics, new needs, new aspirations. You either adapt, or you perish. I think it's worth the effort, if only to get to know the end of the story.

Ten commandments of staying together

○ *Share, right from the start, and I mean such things as housework (soul-destroying, boring), looking after babies and infants (incredibly tiring) and cooking.* Men are supposed to be good cooks, so give your husband the chance to show his skill at the culinary arts. Begin with beans on toast, if he pleads ignorance, and lead him on to better things. If you cosset him in the first months, the first years of marriage, wait on him hand and foot, God help him when you—seeing sense—try to retrain him later on. Do, please, think about and *discuss* together job allocation and *start as you mean to go on.* There's not much point in complaining later that you seem to have ended up as a skivvy.

○ *Reward each other.* If your husband washes the dishes—or your wife the kitchen floor—give him or her lots of *gros baisers:* great big kisses. People tend to criticise, shout at each other when things go wrong; they forget to praise, reward each other when things are going right. Don't forget to congratulate each other, tell each other how marvellous you are. Nobody can live without any praise, any appreciation. Everybody needs stroking.

○ *Write up your allocated tasks on a notice board where you can both see them.* No shilly-shallying. Certain nasty or deadly dull jobs—eg, clearing rubbish, doing the ironing or, for those without green fingers, doing the garden—have to be done. If you do them all, you're a saint, a mug, or a martyr. None of these are easy people to live with. Discuss; post on bulletin board; do. Have a monthly conference to discuss money, chores, and any complaints. If you don't, all you'll breed, besides kids, is resentment.

○ *Disabuse your husband of the quaint notion that children are a woman's affair.* Take turns getting out of bed to see if the baby's still there. Men are quite capable—with help and perseverence—of giving a baby its bottle, changing a nappy. Persevere. The principle is important. Let *him* look after the infants while you go to an evening class. Do leave him with the children for a weekend. There's no finer way to puncture the arrogance of the man who comes home to a wife with young children and tells her, "I've had a terrible day in the office." On your bike, Tarzan. Who's kidding whom? Nothing compares with kids for zap-destroying potential. Later, with Parent/Teacher Associations, get a babysitter and both go, or take it in turns since—here we go again—*children are the responsibility of both parents.* Both should share in the hard work and both should share in the fun. Don't shut your man out; bring him in. It's better for all of you.

○ *Accept change, be flexible, both in your roles and in your relationships.* Romance will wax and wane, but the vital element in any relationship is *friendship,* so talk to each other, tell each other your worries, your hopes, your fears, your little moments of triumph. That's what real friends do, as they grow old and shrink together.

○ *Stay a person yourself.* Don't sacrifice your all to your spouse. Nobody wants the sacrificial bit. Have some fun yourself, keep plenty of friendships going outside of your woosome twosome and family. No output without input; if you martyr yourself over the kitchen stove, you'll have nothing to give to anybody. You're not

Joan of Arc, you're you, so insist on having a circle of companions outside of the family. The family is a safe base, not a prison.

○ *Be realistic about marriage.* It was never meant to provide *all* our intellectual, social, and emotional needs. Doing things for and with others, in the wider community, is vital to our mental health. The best way to become depressed is to stay within four walls. The best antidote to depression is to get out, make new friends, and use the home for a base, not a permanent retreat.

○ *Grow old disgracefully.* Don't use marriage as an excuse for eating boxes of chocolates, losing your figure—or your razzamataz. Develop your spirit, your own personality, using the family as background—despite the demands of the kids. Nobody wants a cardboard cut-out for a spouse (or for a mother or father, come to that).

○ *Live every day.* Marriage isn't a moratorium on living. It's an institution that provides for *some* basic needs (eg, shelter, food, sex). Having met those needs, get on with being the best you can be, becoming more fully yourself. That's a basic need, too.

○ *Keep a sense of humour about it all.* Rows, fights, arguments will come your way. Don't forget those *gros baisers* when you make up. WC Fields said of death that, on the whole, he'd rather be in Philadelphia. You could say that marriage is better than a wet afternoon in Barnsley. Did I hear somebody say only just? It means that you're taking it all too seriously.

Growing with your family

They fell in love, married, bought a little house, and lived happily ever after. Nothing would please me more than to present an Ideal Picture of family life: a father and mother loving each other, two lovely children, a goldfish, and nary a word spoken in anger. For most of us it isn't like that, I'm afraid. The family can be a breeding ground for compassion, friendship, love; it can also be the setting for pain, jealousy, and hate—a living hell. The ideal of a loving family is inspiring,a goal we aim for; it's the reality of family life which is so often disappointing.

These days, I'm not even sure what a family—a group of people living together in one household—consists of. It used to be husband, wife and children under the same roof; now, it could be a woman (or a man) living alone with the children; a group of women living with their offspring; a woman, her partner, plus the kids of both; a man, *his* partner, plus the kids of both, or either. It could be a commune where a number of adults live together and share the mothering and fathering. "Children need mothering and fathering. It doesn't have to come from their mothers and fathers," a colleague once told me. It's an interesting thought.

All we can say with any certainty about families is that they'll thrive where there are lots of Good Moments for every member of the group, where everyone gets some rewards (as well as doing some of the dirty work), and where it isn't *too* boring. People will put up with an incredible amount of drudgery—and housework, for most people, *is* drudgery—if there are some rewards. If there are no rewards, if there is no affection, no friendship, then people will start to look around and wonder whether they ought to chase the blue-bird of happiness elsewhere.

The social setting of the family has changed. Forty years ago, the extended family—with grandparents, uncles, aunts and cousins, plenty of them, living nearby—was the order of the day. As a boy, I lived in the same road as two of my aunts; within walking distance were my other relatives. It was a tribal set-up; both my father and mother came from families of a dozen children. Those relatives provided a ready-made web of social relationships; in case of tragedy, disaster or just plain loneliness, they were *there,* close at hand. I was never lonely as a child, although I rarely saw my parents. People asked less of the family. It was seen as part of a larger, extended unit.

A word of caution, though. I'm sure that, even in the extended family, there was a great deal of cruelty, of physical and emotional tyranny of men over women. Many wives led lives of constant hard labour, with little reward, only hoping that their children might get something better from life than they themselves had managed. The extended family was never idyllic; it *was* a prophylactic against loneliness and isolation.

Nowadays, with the nuclear family (dad, mum and kids living together in little boxes), there is loneliness. The nuclear family usually lives at some distance from relatives. There is more geographical and social mobility: people move away from their home towns to find jobs, chase promotion, start a new life. The dramas enacted behind those closed curtains do not usually spill out on to the streets. The nuclear family pits itself against the world, and the world is a very big place. You'll need help to fight that kind of battle.

The solution, of course, is that neighbours and friends should provide the social nexus, the support system. Friends should take the place of relatives as people we can share our troubles with. Companionship becomes vital as the old social patterns break down, as mobility increases. Yet many people—especially young mothers—lack someone to talk to, someone to confide in. Their own mothers probably live miles away. Many of them try to cope alone. That's an almost impossible task. The slings and arrows of life are difficult to face from the isolation of a semi-detached.

Children are harder work today. When grannies and other relatives lived nearby, when the roads were safe (and when there was less violence, fewer child molesters about), the children could be sent off *somewhere.* Young children could be given to granny to mind, or to older children to look after. If a young mother wanted advice about her baby, there was plenty available from people she knew. Nowadays, a lot of mothers seek advice from "experts". The mother isn't so certain that what she is doing is right: she becomes anxious, lacks confidence, quickly gets demoralised. Don't assume that having six children is any harder than having two. If the social structure were supportive, it could be just as easy. In the old days, mothers had a ready-made support system, a framework of folklore, beliefs, and practical advice to help them through life, to help them live out the major themes of copulation, birth, death. Now, we have to make it up as we go along. That's *much* harder.

The other thing that's changed, besides the social context of the family, is expectation: we all expect more out of life. Take women. After two thousand years of subjugation and domestic slavery, few women now are content to stay within four walls, knitting and sewing, looking after the children. There has been an explosion in the nuclear family, I suspect, simply because more and more women insist on being treated as real people. Fewer women are prepared to act Olive to some man's version of Popeye, or the scullery maid to some latter-day Old Jolyon. The times, they are a changin' and men—many of whom are afraid of women—are baffled when they come across women with minds of their own, women who refuse to settle for a walk-on part in the little domestic drama. In every human relationship there is negotiation, a trade-off. Women, these days, want *more.* Who can blame them?

I think we all want more. Years ago, I remember, an elderly couple won a huge amount of money on the football pools. "What are you going to do with all that cash?" a radio interviewer asked them. "We're going to have a day out in Mablethorpe," said the old lady. No mention of Nice, new fridge/freezer, Rolls Royce. Blessed are they that expect little, for they shall never be disappointed. Nowadays, we expect a lot: from consumer durables to emotional and sexual satisfaction. Nothing wrong with that. It just requires more co-operation between partners, more saying to each other what it is you do want. If the two of you don't keep the channels of communication open these days, the road will be strewn with land-mines, not roses.

Human beings are most peculiar, we seem to be capable of having conflicting needs at one and the same time. We need safety, security, a feeling of belonging, continuity. We also need excitement, new experiences, ecstasy. We are born curious, we need to explore. To embark on family life—especially when you start having children—is to give up a lot. A young woman who has given up a good job and freedom to have a baby will know exactly what I'm talking about. Life's like a restaurant; you have to choose. You can't say to the waiter, "I'll have the lot." You may point to your child, mixing syrup and cornflakes on the kitchen floor, and ask, "Is this it? Did I choose this?" You did indeed, and presumably nobody was twisting your arm while you were choosing.

All of us have other people to consider. His mother or yours, your partner, the kids. Hell is other people, according to Sartre. It isn't really. Hell is inside you, or isn't, according to how well you can balance your own needs against the needs of others. Other people can be a pain in the neck. Often we find it appalling to live with them; yet we can't live without them. Not to consider other people is to risk isolation, loneliness. The fear of loneliness is very powerful. At the same time, we want to do our own thing, be ourselves, be creative, be real. The only solution is to live with compatible people but to be self-centred at the same time (which is not the same thing as being selfish). Be real, insist on your rights, never play Florence Nightingale or Anna Freud. Then, in any group, you are giving *yourself*. That's worth giving.

To live with other people means compromise, or conflict. Adapt or perish, I said of marriage. The same is true of the family. Very rarely, in any family, can we have exactly what we want, when we want it. We have to take into account the equally valid needs of others. Yet we want to come out of the mêlée a real person, a genuine human being, alive, optimistic, life-affirming—not crushed and disintegrated by the roles and the games that others would force us to play.

Then there is the problem of dependency. All human beings are dependent upon other human beings to some extent, even if it's only for daily delivery of the mail or the milk. Few of us want a suffocating, symbiotic dependency, two minds entwined as one, so that neither has room to breathe, neither has any real psychological space. We all know these marital Siamese twins, and sometimes it's sheer lack of courage, the refusal to be a real individual in oneself, that keeps them together, leaning on each other like two broken columns—and about as stable.

At the same time, if we insist on complete independence, we run the risk that all the good things happen elsewhere, outside the home, away from the partner. We then have to face up to some hard questions. *Do I know this person? Do I like this person? Is there any point in staying?* If the answer is a triple no, then that's the end of the marriage. Dependency is inevitable in a close relationship, but it can be a defined dependency rather than an excuse not to stand on our own two feet.

Remember Jenny and Maurice? Let's take up the threads of their family life and see how Maurice is coping with Jenny's insistence on being a person in her own right, as well as being a mother. I would hate you to think that Jenny rebelled, M saw the light and adapted, and everybody lived happily ever after. It wasn't as simple as that. It never is. Compromise, give and take, you-scratch-my-back, lie at the heart of politics; they're often—together with friendship and affection—very prominent within successful families, too.

To Jenny. About two years after The Crisis, I found her in the garden, hanging out the washing and talking to a rosebush. "How does the meadow-flower its bloom unfold?" I heard her declaim, and then—pegging up a pair of jeans and answering her own question—"Because the lovely little flower is free/Down to its root, and, in that freedom, bold." She reached into the plastic washing basket for a shirt. "How's it going today?" I asked. It was going very well. I left her singing away to the trees and went inside to talk to Maurice.

He was sitting in the living-room, head in hands, looking at the television which wasn't switched on. Not a good sign. To cheer Maurice up, I told him that my first wife had died of poisoned mushrooms. "Really?" he said, in a somewhat preoccupied way. "My second wife died of a fractured skull," I told him. He didn't respond. "She wouldn't eat the mushrooms," I explained. "I think," said Maurice, stirring in the armchair, "that Jenny's having an affair." So that was it. Big-Type Crisis Number Two coming up.

A woman, some people say, needs a man to make her heart go *thump*, a man who makes it worthwhile to keep (or regain) her figure. Apparently, Jenny had found a man at the hospital (an administrator, not a patient) who could perform both functions. She was embarking on her first extra-marital affair. Let me say here and now that few women (not to mention men) can embark on, carry through, and end an EMA successfully. Some people claim that women tend to become too wrapped up in, too emotionally dependent upon, too much in love with the man in question. Some say that men simply haven't the stamina for a full-blooded affair. My own view is that most EMAs are doomed simply because of the Rigours of Life. The moving finger writes and, with EMAs, tends to stick itself firmly up one's left nostril.

If I ask Cedric about affairs, he mysteriously quotes Yeats. "Things fall apart; the centre cannot hold," quoth he. I have myself noticed a certain amount of entropy and a fair amount of confusion as to how to expend the limited amount of energy that's available to cope with the family, not to speak of having to save up the zap to cover one's lover's upturned face with burning kisses. To have an extra-marital affair (especially if one has children) is, not to put too fine a point on it, to be a juggler at the feast of life trying to keep four balls in the air at the same time as voices off keep inquiring about their clean underwear. We can all learn to juggle; it's having to service dependents at the same time that defeats most of us.

Eschew philosophy: consider the practicalities of Having An Affair. First, somewhere to meet. This isn't always easy to find. Many's the woman who's found that the park-keeper (or car-park attendant) is in the same darts club as her husband. It's hard to know what to say if, sitting in the Morris 1000 with your Ideal Man, a face appears at the window and a voice says, "Cyril's missus, isn't it? Children got over the measles?" I know a woman who met her lover in a tiny village in Devon; there, in a restaurant, holding hands with The Vision, she noticed her boss at a corner table. "Have you met my brother?" she asked him, when he came over. I won't tell you the knots that crept into this little scenario when the boss met the husband the following week. If a tiny village in the next county isn't safe, think of the risks you take when the lights go up in the local cinema and you're there in the back row nibbling his ear. There are places where lovers can meet in safety—Sark, Umbria, Lesbos—providing that you have the time and the money. Even your husband is bound to ask, if you disappear for a few days and come back sun-tanned and flushed with excitement, why it's taken you so long to get the morning paper.

Some might argue that this desperate search for privacy becomes far less fraught if you are open and honest with your spouse about what's going on. Fair enough. That's what Jenny thought. She got to the bit that always makes me smile: Total Honesty. I've never seen it work yet. It didn't work with Jenny. She told Maurice everything; she told M about Teddy (Jenny is drawn to men with appalling names) and how nice he was, that he was in admin, but was very poetic, and that poetry was a common love, and how he was happily married himself and was in no way a threat to the marriage. No, it wasn't just friendship. They had *done it*—slept together, or at least, made love, twice—although it wasn't very comfortable or sexually all that exciting. Total honesty.

I think Jenny had guessed that Maurice had become more than slightly paranoid about the whole scene. He had, and she'd suspected it, started following her about in his car. Jenny thought that was awful, undignified, sick. She wanted to allay his jealousy, reassure him that she cared about him, never wanted to hurt him. That's why she decided upon the Confessional.

That's when Maurice hit her, beat her up. "He went completely mad," she told me. "Really battered me. I was afraid for my life." I felt ashamed of Maurice, but I wasn't surprised. Sexual jealousy is a powerful emotion. Many men are phallus-oriented; the thought that somebody, somewhere, may be more potent, more virile, than themselves is hard to take. If Jenny had said, "It was not worth doing sexually, that's not what it was about," Maurice would have asked, "Then why did you do it?" If she had said it was marvellous sexually, I believe that he would have done her real physical harm. It was bad enough as it was. The truth of the matter was that Maurice at that time went round the bend, temporarily mad.

Having failed to find Somewhere To Do It (other than the office floor, at lunchtime), and having failed to convince Maurice that it was All Right To Do It, Jenny had her third failure: so keen was she on (a) Real Romance and (b) Being Affirmed As A Worthwhile, Attractive Person that she became very intense with Teddy, told *him* what had happened, and made him feel guilty about the whole wretched business. Jenny failed to see that her confessions might be something of a luxury, not so much a sign of integrity as a need to ease her own conscience. She went for Teddy like a bull goes for a gate, and he cooled off: the poetry was forgotten; the reality started to seep in. Jenny took her frustrations out on the children, and on Maurice. Meanwhile he stopped beating her up. They talked and talked and talked. They stayed up until four in the morning, sometimes, talking. They went on long walks, and talked. They talked in the kitchen, and in bed. I think they were trying to salvage something from the emotional wreckage of Jenny's desperate Bid For Individuality and Freedom.

Maybe they were lucky, maybe they just worked at it really hard. Jenny gave up Teddy, not because of M but because it simply wasn't working, it had ceased to be romantic. M and J came to a Great Decision together. There would be Less Talk, Less Analysis, Less Picking Over The Bones of Living. There would be More Space. If either wanted to go out, so be it. No questions. If life-enhancing experiences were to happen to either of them, they were to grasp the LEEs and decide as adults how to handle the problems that arose. No probing, no discussion. More trust, less inquisition. Maurice, in fact, was doing the only thing he could do to save his marriage: he saw that Jenny must take moral responsibility for her own existence.

What happened next is interesting. Jenny cooled it and Maurice started with Phase II of Becoming a Human Being. She stopped looking for somebody as though she had to prove something to herself. She did go out (and I know that once a month she had a mysterious assignation in the small country town of X; she said it was to go to the market but I happen to know that the market's in the next town along). Jenny possibly had a man-friend, even a lover. I didn't ask her, neither did Maurice. She seemed very happy. She had the freedom to choose, the psychological space to make her own decisions and it really showed in the warm, loving way she related to the children and in the more open and spontaneous way she related to Maurice. He's started going out, too—mind you, only to a drama group, bit parts. But it wasn't with Jenny, it was all by himself. When you've been married for twelve years, even that can take courage. I think that M was slowly learning to re-find his real self, the man that Jenny had married (he must have had *something*), and he was learning to lean less on Jenny emotionally. The price had been high: the showdown, the nasty bits, the violence. Was it worth it? I'm not certain. They're still together. They seem to be reasonably happy in their relationship. That, at this juncture, is all that I can say. Time will tell.

Perhaps we are condemned to live through these things before we really understand them. If you can't hear, you have to feel; if you experience it, you get the point. I still think that we can benefit from the experiences of others. What Jenny and Maurice learned so painfully can be grasped by other, especially younger, couples without them having to go through all that agony. The vital lesson is the importance of mutual respect, of space, of generosity, of trust. You must watch out for problems of boundary maintenance (you keep to your patch, this is mine, and this is the patch we share together); you must be aware of fantasy projections and destructive, regressive games; you must avoid those barbarous assaults on your partner's integrity and dignity. You must be optimistic and believe that, despite daily demands, constraints, and aggravations, many people navigate the treacherous shores of family life to reach the native shores of their own being. It takes determination, as well as a good recipe book, to make a dish that's worth the eating.

I've said little about children. Let's talk about them. Why not? After all, even though you will be striving to be *real*, you can hardly reprimand your child, "Quintin, you're invading my psychological space." After children, I want to talk about fathers, only because I feel sorry for a great many men these days. I think a lot of them haven't got tickets to the Great Feast of Life and are outside there, peering in through the window.

Children are sent forth as living arrows to bring adults down to reality, and to puncture any ideas they may have about Gracious Living. They are the human fire extinguishers of randy feelings, the scourge of self-determination, an ever-present trouble in time of our own emotional needs. Children can also be very nice, great fun, good company. If we've got them, we chose to have them.

The trick, for a child, is to pick the right mum. Some mothers are super-mums; they breeze along (here a cream cracker, there a cuddle) without any trouble at all. Super-mums either fill you with admiration or make you want to spit. I shan't take up any time on them. They don't need me.

This is addressed to average mums and dads—like you and me—who find bringing up children very hard work. With mums, the trick is to pick the right dad. There's no law that says it's solely the mother's duty to bring up the kids. It should be a shared enterprise. It often isn't; that only makes it far more excruciatingly gruelling than if *two* parents are involved. To take on the responsibility for children when you're isolated, alone, is to give yourself a *very* hard time and to risk exhaustion.

What is it that is so tiring about children, especially young children? That's easy. It's being with them *all the time* that shatters you. The solution is to institute more convivial contexts for mothering: "cuppa clubs", mother and toddler groups, a neighbourhood group of mums getting together and talking, comparing experiences, while their children play. You'll find you're not the only one who doesn't find it all plain sailing. You'll discover that you're not the only mum who's twitchy, whose child won't sleep, whose husband never lifts a finger. It doesn't solve your problems, but it helps you to share them. It's easier—or should be—for a woman with a baby in a pram to make friends. It's vital she should do. Those new friends have to give the support which, in the old days, was provided by relatives. Mothering is a community activity. It was never meant to be done alone.

There is no universal mother instinct. If you don't get any satisfaction out of mothering, you may have to face up to your infant being better off with a registered child minder, while you go out to office, factory, or wherever gives you the financial and emotional rewards you need. You may not have any choice in the matter; many young mothers *have* to work. The evidence is that no child is ever damaged by being left during the day with a good child minder. My advice? Take your time. You and dad can make a few inquiries; find the right minder for your child. It's worth it for the child's sake, and for your own peace of mind.

At the age of three, the child can be taken along to the local preschool playgroup. I have a lot of time for the playgroup movement. It *involves* mothers in the socialisation of their own children. This is very important. It is nearly always mum who orchestrates her child's learning. The boundaries of the mother become the boundaries of the child; it is mum who teaches the child to sing—or squawk—life's song. Just as important, the pre-school playgroup gives mother a chance to meet other mums, to talk, learn, compare notes. It's the right idea, again: mothering as a community enterprise. I know. What about *dads?* Don't fret. I shall get around to those blighters in a moment.

As children grow up, you mustn't look for trouble. Children, of whatever age, need action. You need a bit of peace. The solution is to get them out of your hair. Show them affection, be responsive when you are with them; listen to them, talk to them—but remember that they don't want you (or you them) all the time. Get out there and find out what's going on in the community. If nothing exists, start something up. There is always a need for parents to help out with resource groups, community workshops, holiday play schemes, youth clubs; if nothing exists in your neighbourhood for children and teenagers, get together with a few people and see if you can start something going. Motherhood (and fatherhood) is far less demanding and much more fun when it's shared with others. You'll probably be brilliant with other people's children; I am—it's my own that seem to get on my nerves.

Teenagers in particular need action—and room to breathe, the feeling that they are not being psychoanalysed, watched, criticised the whole time. They have to become adults. It isn't easy if your parents insist upon treating you as a fussy child, or as the Beast from Five Fathoms.

With teenagers, it's essential to stay a person yourself. You have to make sacrifices for them, but don't sacrifice yourself *to* them. They want to look across the room at a real person—and that means that you'll argue, disagree, have differences of opinion, go through periods of disliking each other, just like real people. It's vital not to be a martyr. Your home *isn't* a hotel. They should lend a hand. If you take it as natural that they should and pin up the job roster each month, everybody will be more inclined to muck in than if you do everything for them and then rant and rave when you discover that they're taking advantage of you.

The generation gap can be bridged more easily if you remember that teenagers want new experiences, new challenges, status, a bit of recognition, and a chance to exercise responsibility for somebody else or for something (needs very similar to our own). Those youngsters below the emotional poverty line will tend to make their mark not in good personal relationships but with aerosol cans. In the home, negotiation works better than Do-It-Or-Else. The trouble with DIOE is that (a) it doesn't work, (b) it creates an atmosphere in the house which suggests that the Third World War is imminent and (c) it isn't a very good preparation for adult life, in which we have to learn to negotiate and to respect the needs of others.

Teenagers have always rebelled and *will* always rebel against adults; this is part of their need to be different, independent, interesting. Recently, I went through a swearing patch. "Oh, I say!" said my own teenagers; they started to speak like BBC news readers—just to be different. Since teenagers sometimes have the annoying habit of rejecting what their elders say or do, we can use this tendency to our own advantage. For instance, since I started to look scruffy, my son has appeared immaculate; since I started imitating his way of speaking—rather like a Tibetan Yak—he has begun speaking very quickly and wittily like Noel Coward.

This see-saw effect, known as the Iron Filings Law (you go south, they go north) is worth committing to memory. When I was a lad, a friend of mine fell in love with her cousin. She was forbidden to bring the boy to the house, or to see him. Needless to say, she eventually married him. If the parents had played it my way ("Do bring him round, I'm sure he'll love your father's stories about his pigeons and his experiences in the Pioneer Corps in the last war"), the chap would probably have taken off and never come back, and my friend would have married a non-relative out of spite.

I've seen some hardcore teenagers in my time, and picked up the pieces of shattered family relationships, sometimes too late. "My daughter shouts, criticises me, drinks, smokes, and goes out with a fifty-year-old Armenian with a wooden leg. Is this normal?" What is one to say? I have no idea how many Armenians have wooden legs. This is a slight exaggeration, I know, but the war between the generations can be very dramatic and very tragic. I always wonder whether the trouble sets in early with the parents' failure to realise that (a) it's better to talk than to fight and (b) it's better to listen than to talk. A good pair of ears beats a blazing row, or a too-ready tongue, every time.

These days teenagers have more money than we had, and more sexual freedom. They also have more choices to make in a world that is bewildering, rapidly changing, often uncaring. Who can envy teenagers today, with their problems—including, for many, unemployment—and the perennial anxieties of tits and/or pimples and the impression that they are creating on others? If somebody asked me if I'd like to be a teenager again, I'd say, "No, thanks!" All that self-consciousness, awkwardness, self-doubt. Talk to the teenagers you know and you'll be surprised how pleasant they are and how confused and lonely they are—just like you. It shouldn't be Us and Them.

A word about unemployment. Not to work eats away at the soul. Not many of us could put up with being totally idle for more than a fortnight. It's vital that we do something about unemployed teenagers. They want, most of all, jobs. They deserve a chance to work for a living. If we find that in our area jobs are hard to come by, then it is up to us to create community schemes and to offer recreational opportunities to teenagers not at work. Not to work is, for most young people who have left school, a tragedy. Unemployment leads to lethargy and despair. It creates anti-social attitudes, cynicism, depression and, in some cases, crime. *It is up to the adults in the community to do something about it.* They owe it to the young people.

To sound a cheerful note, I have to admit that I've thoroughly enjoyed the company of my own children as teenagers. It's been great fun and very interesting. My daughter's first boyfriend was a shock. ("I wouldn't want to breed from that chap," I whispered to my wife in bed after meeting him.) Discussing sex before marriage with my daughters, sex after marriage with my son. When my daughter went away to Paris for a year, I was worried sick. I didn't tell *her* that. That's part of the worry. The worry you can put up with if, just occasionally, you have some fun together or at least see each other as friends.

Now, to dads. One of the biggest changes that has come about in the family over the last half-century is in the Role of Father. At one time, dad had a formal, in-built authority. He didn't have to be charismatic; you had to do as he said whether you liked him or not. He was the family money box; the purse strings were in his hand, held tightly in a clenched fist. A child who defied father risked a severe beating; so did a wife. A wife risked being thrown out on the streets, penniless. The financial and physical tyranny was a very real—and terrifying—thing.

The toll of two world wars, the decline of the Heavenly Father, the peripatetic nature of families, the loss of faith in father-figure politicians (at the time of writing this we have a woman prime minister at last) and most crucial of all, the ever-growing awareness and expectations of women (and their demands that they be treated as people rather than servants and/or sex objects), all represent a massivc social upheaval. Many women have found a voice, a role in the wider community, an executive as well as, or instead of, a nurturing function. Must it be that as women gain confidence, men will automatically become even more frightened of them? Just what is the man's role in the family, what his relationship with his wife?

To take these questions in reverse order, the man should be a friend and a companion to his spouse. As a friend, he's very useful in the family: besides bringing in an income (single mothers *are,* on average, much worse off than married women), he is another adult around the place, somebody to talk to, somebody to say "bless you" when you sneeze, someone to hold your hand if you're troubled, scratch your back if it's itchy. He can help with the children, do his share, take on some of the drudgery of the home, share joys, sorrows, housework, and child-minding with his spouse. Some husbands do take a full share in the rearing of the children, and in the routine tasks of the home. A husband *can* be a friend, a pearl beyond price.

Some husbands, it must be admitted, are neither friend nor ornament. They see their role as the hunter, going out, exploring the world, while the little woman stays back in the cave with their children, the cooking pots, and the nappies. This division of labour might have made sense when women had a dozen children each, when women ran the household, grew the vegetables, tended the poultry while men worked from dawn till dusk in the fields and with the livestock. Women, then, had no choice. Nor did men. Now, we all have a choice.

Some women (but not many) earn more than men; some men are on social security, while their wives go out to work; some women simply don't find enough satisfaction in running a home, bringing up children. How is a man to insist that the wife stay by the hearth in her traditional role when her traditional tasks have been taken over by the men who provide tinned food, battery hens, and mass-produced clothing? Men who wish to play Tarzan are having more and more difficulty these days in finding women who are willing to play Jane. More women want to go out and bring back some bananas for themselves. They want no part of a master/servant relationship; at least on the farm it was a partnership, even if an unequal one. Women want justice.

Some men do not have the flexibility. They'll try to insist on the age-old Me Tarzan/You Jane dichotomy. The only trouble with this is that it doesn't work. Tyranny is no substitute for democracy; domination is no substitute for negotiation. Women have begun to realise that a marriage in which they get no rewards, no justice, no emotional satisfaction just isn't worth the candle. In the old days men deserted women. Now, more and more, women are deserting men. Is it surprising that the divorce rate is moving rapidly upwards? Adapt or perish. A lot of men won't adapt. The family, in an increasing number of cases, perishes.

Most women prefer to have a man about the house. They would also prefer that man not to be violent, feckless, an absentee landlord. They don't want brutes, fools, insensitive louts. They want somebody they can talk to, be friends with, and if they don't find any gratification in the family, women are more and more prepared to look elsewhere. To cope with these new demands, men resort to various strategies: violence, getting a job that entails less contact with the home (fathers on paper, but rarely at home, and certainly not in the family spiritually or emotionally), financial blackmail, bluster, resorting to yet more macho pursuits. It doesn't work. The problems are too important to go away or to be solved by simple expedients. In a school I know, one out of seven children doesn't have a father living at home. They may have an "uncle"—the woman's present partner—or they may have a relative of the mother living there. Some children will miss their father desperately. Other children will be quite happy, providing mother is making out, providing that she is a viable human being. "We're better off without him," one girl said to me of her father. Many families might not be financially, but are emotionally, socially and spiritually. Having dispensed with a man who is a brute, a fool, a lout, they can respond to the challenge of life, be themselves, and hope for the best. *With* father, the best is out of the question.

It's very sad, in a way. When I first started writing about children I used to tell of mum and dad, 2.4 beautiful kids, humorous incidents—which were true enough. Mother in Laura Ashley dress, entertaining guests. "Mummy's got no knickers on," whispers her little girl to the handsome man from the office. "My mummy's twenty-one," a little boy told me. "How old's your big sister?" I asked. "Twelve." Even in the clinic, twenty years ago, I used to write on the case notes, "This mother looks anxious." I've since realised that *all* mothers look anxious. Now, I try to write the truth. My picture of The Happy Family has changed over the years. For one thing, I've come to realise that it's possible to have a happy family without dad. Many women I know are single parents. They *are* making out; they *are* happier than they were as a housewife; their children *aren't* disturbed, miserable.

The sad bit is the rejected man. He's like the dinosaur, roaming about, making a loud noise, looking for somebody to tread on, but there are few creatures left who are daft enough to stand around and be trodden on. It's tough on him. Macho man is doomed to extinction: there's a diminishing market for muscle. Women would prefer to live with a sensitive man, a sympathetic woman, in a commune, or by themselves rather than live with *him.* He's not needed any more. Macho man is out. "Mum, the garbage man is here." "Tell him we don't need any." Women don't want garbage. They don't want macho men, cheats, Tarzans. They do need friendship, justice, to be treated as real people. That is what family life is all about. You treat each other with consideration, as friends, or you create an emotional wilderness in which you go to the wall.

Partnership is the answer, but there are going to be many more tears before some of us get anywhere near it. I believe that things will get better for families—and especially for women. In America there have been surveys which show that women there are happier than they used to be. They've paid a price—in emotional turmoil, in sheer courage against the odds—for their newly found freedom. It would be silly to suggest that, say, working-class wives in this country are anywhere near freedom, have any choice, are at any time very far away from severe depression. But things will get better for *all* women. Women have glimpsed the searchlight of freedom flickering over the sea of exploitation. There's nothing, in my view, which will stop the ship of women's rights making its slow way towards the harbour of justice.

You'll see, now, that Jenny and Maurice aren't doing too badly. They're learning to give each other space. They're learning, slowly, that nobody's been able to invent a better institution than the family to bring up children, but that the family is an organic thing—something that changes, grows—and that the nuclear family is no good without emotional and social support systems. The family has to grow in the soil of the wider community; unless it has the light provided by the outside world, the world of companionship and friendship, it withers and dies. What holds the rickety parcel of family life together is the string of love. We can only truly love people if they give us room to breathe, space to grow, to develop, to do our own thing. Love is *not* possessing somebody.

Why lock yourself in? It's your own fault if you do. There's a big wide world out there composed of ordinary, lonely people—just like you. Why not go out and meet them? More and more people, finding family life a prison, will walk out—but they'll be looking for some kind of family, some group, in which to live out their lives.

Family life needn't be a gaol cell. It can be very enjoyable, but only if you see the community as its context and insist that you're willing to give of your best if others give of themselves, too. Start as you mean to go on, don't build the prison round yourself. When you start a family, you don't begin a life sentence, you set off on an adventure. Be careful whom you set off with, grow together, and don't forget to have some fun together along the way.

Survival kit for family life

○ *Sort things out before you start a family.* Would you, having given up a well-paid job to have children, have to ask him for money for a new pair of jeans? And how about if *he* gives up a job to look after the family—would you then feel that you had the upper hand as the breadwinner? Negotiate all this well in advance of the patter of tiny feet. Set an allowance if only one partner stays home, a definite proportion of all income (this partnership is mutual, remember?), and don't think in terms of handouts. Money is at the root of a lot of family arguments, so—even if you don't have a written contract—get it all clarified in your minds before the ship sails out of port.

○ *Don't expect too much from the family.* It can't provide for *all* your intellectual, social, and emotional needs. Friends outside the house can, so look for them. If you live your life in a tight little nuclear box, you shouldn't be surprised when it explodes in your face.

○ *Insist on fulfilling your own needs.* Do your thing, keep your style (I know it's hard with a baby mewling and puking all over you). If you decide to have an extra-marital affair in order to regain your freedom, then take the responsibility for yourself. Don't "confess" to ease your own conscience, or because you feel you've done something without asking permission. If you have an affair, make sure it adds to you, and to your family attitudes, and don't forget to take a degree in bus timetables.

○ *Make it clear what your role is.* You're not to be a domestic manager/skivvy/someone who does most of the dirty work. Women are the sex that has babies; that doesn't mean that they have to take total responsibility for looking after them all the time. Get the show on the road, but make it a joint production.

○ *View your family as a growing, ever-changing scenario, not a Victorian tableau with you as the static lady.* It's not a photograph you're in—it's a film, with lots of twists and turns in the plot. It can only have a happy ending if you take part in directing it.

○ *Family life is hard work.* I used to think that all families ever did was to stand around grand pianos singing, or sit, gazing at each other lovingly. I now know it isn't so. In the middle of all the routine and gunge, don't forget rewards. Everybody needs them. Insist on your share of them.

○ *Have rosters, lists of duties.* Leave nothing to chance. The chances are you'll end up at the blunt end of a vacuum cleaner while he's playing golf, or darts, or something equally incomprehensible. Say what you want. Get some justice. It's a useful ointment for easing the pain of family life.

○ *Come out with your grievances.* Cedric's wife asked him on a Wednesday, "Why are you so boring?" She left him on the Friday. They'd been married ten years, and it was unfair. She should have tackled him about it during the honeymoon rather than let it fester all that time.

○ *If you feel depressed, get out of the house as much as possible.* Depression is an occupational hazard with young mothers. Pills won't cure it; starting up a neighbourhood mothers' group, helping at the local playgroup, doing something with other people in the same boat very well might.

○ *As the family grows and evolves, grow yourself.* Otherwise, when your children are older you'll be a cardboard cut-out, pathetically obsessed with kids and cooking. Who wants a two-dimensional woman? It's *your* life, not theirs.

Facing up to change

Butterflies don't have identity problems. It's egg, next caterpillar, then chrysalis and—pow!—butterfly, perfect, not a wrinkle in sight, fluttering about in the sunshine. You don't get bees who come to the edge of the flower and say, "To be a bee, or not to be a bee." They know what they have to be. With us, it's different. We have choice, and none of us is ever quite certain as to how we'll turn out. If we were, there'd be no point in writing this book.

Take, for example, fritillaries. With them, you can observe a complete metamorphosis, a moving towards perfection, a final stage, a completion. It doesn't work like that with humans. Speak for yourself, buster (you might say), I'm on my way to being a Truly Lovely Person; it can't be long now. All I can say is, don't hold your breath. My own theory is that very, very few of us ever make it to maturity, the Lovely Stage, the imago. Many of us have trouble enough in just trying to be adults.

When I was learning to dance, I didn't stick at it long enough to learn to turn round. In a waltz or foxtrot, my partner would end up pressed against the wall at the far end of the hall or flat on her back—tulle all crumpled—among the tables and chairs near the exit. Life's like that. One minute you might look in the mirror and say, "Perfection's not far off." Next minute somebody's treading all over you, and your hand-sewn sequins are scattered far and wide across the ballroom floor.

I very much doubt whether there is a Mid-Life Crisis which is any worse than the crises—the downs and, I hope, ups—that we have to face throughout life. Each ten years of a person's life, as Goethe said, has its own fortune, its own hopes, its own desires. Each decade also has its own heartbreaks, setbacks, crises, problems to be solved. The time to stop living, or to stop battling with life's complexities, is when you stop breathing. We're all in this together, all on the magical mystery tour, and none of us ever quite makes it to the Grand Metamorphosis. If great changes happen to us—spiritual *or* emotional—they can happen at any stage along the road. If disaster strikes, it can strike at any time, any place. The main thing to remember is that you can make the good moments happen at any age from nine to ninety.

This theme of a *continuous search for authenticity*—a never-ending search for our inner core, fulfilment—is not affected by what seems to me to be a very arbitrary and misleading concept: chronological age. The date of birth on their passports is no guide to how people behave. I know people of twenty-eight who act as though they were fifty. I know senior citizens who trot about, laugh, giggle, and chatter like thirteen-year-olds. Nana, my wife's grandmother, went out with a man of eighty-six when she was ninety-seven. They used to hold hands in the kitchen; she'd wear her special lilac hat when they went on coach rides to Salisbury. They didn't so much have a spark of life as a great roaring fire. The lust for magic, for active life doesn't have anything to do with how old you are. You can be miserable at forty. Life at sixteen can be pretty ghastly, too, sometimes. There are bad bits—and there are also some very good bits—all along the way.

Let's face it, if you're twenty, you'll sometimes wonder what it's like to be thirty, and maybe even worry how to move towards the ripe old age of forty without despair, *Angst*, terror, or the feeling (is that grey hair and I'm still only twenty-five?) that the best thing you can do is head to the nearest duck pond and throw yourself in. Don't worry. I'm forty-odd and I'll tell you the truth. It doesn't necessarily get better as you get older, and it doesn't necessarily get worse. It's up to you. It depends on your attitude, your philosophy, your lust for life, your determination to gather ye rosebuds while ye may until they carry you off in a coffin. We're all going to die. Let's not waste any time worrying about that. It's life that we're interested in here.

In our society there's a great deal of ageism: prejudice against or dislike of people not in the same age group as yourself. It's just as divisive, in my view, as sexism and racism. It prevents people from getting to know each other, benefiting from each other's experience of life; it makes people cluster in their own age groups, mistrust older or younger people. It's phoney. Being interested or being attractive has nothing to do with age. Cliff Richard is past forty: I wouldn't mind having his charisma, or his looks. Paul Newman's pushing on a bit—ditto. Margot Fonteyn, too. Does it matter? The main thing is for people to be in there, giving out, learning what they can about relationships, happiness, at all stages of life. Don't play the numbers game; don't cling to ageist attitudes—get out there and live, whatever your age.

But (you say) as we grow older we lose our looks. That's sexist. If your face is your fortune, you could end up bankrupt. What about my figure? Mine's an utter Things-Fall-Apart, Centre-Cannot-Hold disaster area. I still can't take a defeatist, beauty-queen attitude towards life and relationships. I know women and men with the most awful, punctured-water-bed figures who have the most amazing sex lives. Perhaps it's because they're cheeky; perhaps it's because they know that other people are much too concerned about their own hips, sticky-out ears, bulging tummies, or entropic behinds to worry about anyone else's. The Awful Figure people I've just mentioned smile a lot, talk to people as though they were interested in them. That, I guess, is why they do much better with others than some of the lovely, lonely men and women you see around you every place you go.

Let's have plenty of truth, not too much flannel. The fear of ageing can and *does* terrify lots of people. This terror of Growing Old has, with the folks I know, reached ridiculous proportions. I was walking down our drive and my elder daughter was standing by the front door. "Goodbye, sweet youth," she called out. Was she saying cheerio to her boyfriend? Negative. There was nobody else there. Could she mean me? Unlikely. As young as I look (in the dusk, with the light behind me, I could pass for thirty-nine), nobody would mistake me for a lad. Then I remembered that it was her fifteenth birthday. At this rate, we'll have teenyboppers of ten weeping on each other's shoulders because they've reached double figures.

I'm going to assume here that you will—whether you like it or not, and if you keep out of heavy traffic—reach thirty, forty, and mileposts beyond. The best thing I can do is to tell you about the things that can and do happen to people during mid-life (and I mean anything from thirty to forty-five). Then you can't say that you haven't been informed. What you do, if crisis time hits you at this stage, is still up to you. I just hold the mirror up. You decide whether you see anything of yourself, now or in the future, in the shiny glass. I can't tell you how to handle your crisis when it happens. I can only tell you how other people handled their slings and arrows. If you're *very* young and you tell me later that you recognise nothing of yourself in all this, I can only say what Picasso said when people complained that his portrait of Gertrude Stein didn't look like her. "No matter, it will," said Pablo. If you're twenty, with no problems, all I can say is, "Give it time."

I won't suggest easy solutions; that would be silly. Life isn't all neat and tidy like a box of chocolates; more often, it's like a teenager's bedroom. And I'm not sure, anyway, how useful it is to give specific advice. Read the stories, digest, then do your own thing, is my tip. They may, or may not, apply to you. No point in me, the Great Explorer, telling you how to survive up the Zambesi when you live in Tower Hamlets. Then again, I suppose, we all have our own equivalents (if we haven't they'll come along) of finding ourselves up some emotional Orinoco, without a paddle, without a canoe, and with a distinct feeling that something nasty—or miraculous—is just about to happen. Cautionary Tales coming up.

CASE 1
Within these walls, or the mid-life art of middle-class manners

Meg married a really nice guy. Everybody said how nice Brian was, especially her parents. He had a good job, pleasant manners, a good salary. He was nine years older than she, mature and sincere, and got on well with older people—he would obviously make a wonderful father. "Nice chap," said Meg's dad to Meg's mum as the happy couple wed. Everybody thought so; they still do—even Meg.

She left him when she was thirty-four. It had lasted ten years and she'd just got more and more depressed about the situation. The thing was, he was too perfect, too nice. He never got angry, always understood ("Lord, protect me from understanding, just give me passion," she'd sometimes say to herself in bed), never nagged, washed the dishes, treated her kindly. They had two beautiful boys (everyone said how super they were, and very like their father), no money problems. They had nice furniture, wall-to-wall carpeting, fridge/freezer, and they went to France every year for a two-week holiday. From the outside, looking in, it seemed to be a perfect family. From the inside—from Meg's point of view—it was all the important things (as it slowly dawned on her) that weren't right.

First of all, did she love him? She *liked* him (everybody did; he was so courteous, so considerate), but she wasn't certain she felt any love for him. Why had she married him? Well, she needed, she thought, somebody reliable, as she tended to be a bit scatty, untidy, the arty type. He was a good catch—everybody said so. He was tall, good-looking, well-dressed. Her family adored him. She married him because other people thought he was so suitable; looking back, she couldn't honestly say she'd been in love—she just did what seemed to be the inevitable thing. The marriage had made so many people so happy.

His face. That annoyed her. She liked a bit of asymmetry in faces. His habit of clearing some of the dishes away before the meal was finished, stacking the main course plates neatly in the sink before they had pudding, that annoyed her. Why not finish the meal, relax? To hell with the dishes. She became deliberately untidy—to rile him. He understood. He said women can get run down, weary.

Then there was sex. That, technically, was good. She had her share of orgasms, as the book said was her right and entitlement. He was considerate about that, waited. It was all so lacking in passion, fervour, words. He made a good job of it (he was the sort of man you could rely on to do a good job; she just didn't feel terribly *involved*, that's all). One night, staring up at the ceiling as he was making love to her, she said out loud, "It's all for other people." It was. He had what he wanted; her family—and his—had what they wanted; the boys had what they wanted. Other people had always had what they wanted from her. Others had written the play; she fulfilled her part, said her lines, was a reasonable wife and mother. She couldn't honestly say that she'd had what *she* wanted, not from any of it. If you'd have asked her then, when she was thirty-three, what she did want, she wouldn't have been able to tell you.

The next year it happened, and very quickly. She joined an art class (she had wanted to get a job as a teacher, but Brian had said with his salary there was no need for her to work) and met a man, Dave. He was twenty-six, on the dole, a painter. He said what an interesting face she had and would it be possible for him to come around to the house and paint her portrait? Brian had no objections (he was very understanding). That was the move that lost Brian his queen. Meg fell for Dave. He asked her to run away with him; she left home, children, husband, and fridge/freezer and went to live in a tiny derelict cottage with another couple, four young children, and two labradors. She was deliriously happy. This was the X factor that had been missing. Love. Irrational, stupid, nonsensical love. She loved Dave. That was what *she'd* wanted.

Back at the ranch it was why time. "Why?" asked Brian (he cried, so did the boys). "Why?" asked Meg's father. He didn't understand what Meg could possibly see in a short, spotty, bespectacled, scruffy, unemployed "lout" like Dave (Meg had had the cheek, in the first blush and optimism of love, to take her Loved One home to meet her parents). I could see what she saw in him. For one thing he was, in nearly every way, the opposite of Brian. Meg told me one evening (naughty girl), "Honestly, T, he's absolutely hopeless at sex." She laughed. "I don't mind a bit." She looked radiantly happy. I think it was the very first time in her life that she was actually doing her own thing. "You could always teach him," I said. "Very slowly." I try not to take sides in these matters—and there *was* the question of leaving the boys—but, frankly, Meg was so obviously in love that I found it hard to make any moral judgement on her mid-morning abandonment of hearth and home and her search for meaning, authenticity and—dare I say it?—happiness.

Things with Dave didn't work out. (I *said* life wasn't neat and tidy.) They stayed together for four years, then parted. But she grew, really grew emotionally, in that time. She is with another man now. Brian's married again. The boys are happy; Meg still sees them regularly, loves them more now, thinks about them a lot. She isn't quite sure whether she would do the same thing again. On balance, considering what Brian was like—and there is no arguing about her subjective truth, her negative feelings towards him—she reckons she would. Things with her new man, touch wood, are fine at the moment. She's a great girl, Meg. "Seems peculiar, doesn't it, to grow up when you're in your thirties? It's a bit late, isn't it?" That's what she said to me. I don't think it's peculiar at all. Some people grow up when they're forty, or fifty, or sixty. Some lucky ones are growing all the time. Some people don't grow up at all. Better to find out what you want late than go through life and never find it.

Analysis of case 1

You don't, unless you're really looking for trouble and determined to hurt yourself, marry somebody because your parents, your Aunt Edna, your old Uncle Albert, or your friends think he (or she) is suitable/a jolly good catch/terribly good-looking. You do marry somebody because *you* like and/or love him or her. That should be obvious, but it doesn't always happen.

Pick a man as you'd pick a pudding from the selection on the sweet trolley: because you like that kind of thing, not because people are whispering in your ear that the cheesecake is superb. It may be for them, with their palates, but that doesn't mean that *you* will like it. Go by your own instincts. That's what we were given instincts for. (If you're older, reading this, you'll know it's true; this is mainly addressed to younger readers who'll also know it's true but may not always have the courage to resist social pressures or the confidence to follow their hearts.)

Let's have a few words here on the nature of love and on what Abraham Maslow, an American psychologist, called D (deficiency) love and B (being) love. Love is a vital need. We all know that. When we love, when we are loved, we don't use up love—we give out *more* love. Love breeds love, just as unhappiness, despair, and loneliness breed unhappiness, despair, and loneliness. The practical point is that we can't *use* love to cure ourselves of some pathological condition, to fill some gaping hole at the centre of our being. With love, it's the other who is important; B love, the only real love, is a love for the Being, the essence, of the other. It's unheeding; it's unselfish; it's not concerned with carpets, money, a nice house, a higher material standard of living. The higher standard of living is in the emotions, in the heart; the rewards are intangible, but they are many. Real love, as I've said before, is a privilege—not a duty.

You don't take a person and have a relationship (or marry) in order to cure something—as if you were taking medicine to cure a cold. It doesn't work. Unless you love and like the other person, you have very little chance of curing anything at all. I suspect that Meg married Brian because she wanted (a) to live away from her parents, (b) a project (ie, starting a family) that would take up her time, and (c) somebody to look after her. That's very understandable. It isn't love. It's using somebody to fill up a gap, a deficit, in your relationship. Much better to work towards a time when you're reasonably happy and, from that position of happiness, look for somebody who can share in your own feelings of love.

B love's the best love. It's enjoyable, non-possessive, and alive. It grows rather than shrinking or disappearing. It's an end in itself, not a means of getting a dishwasher or shot of your parents. It's like looking at a beautiful painting: you can't say just why it gives you so much pleasure, but there's no denying the fact that it does. B love makes you feel happy, aware: you notice birds singing, you smile at people more; it's therapeutic, not crippling. There's little pay-off in terms of more specific gratifications, from new clothes to vacuum cleaners to orgasms. You just feel better, that's all. You want to get to know the other person *more*—not less—with B love; you don't feel aggressive/hostile or anxious/dependent, just happier; you feel more than an individual, not less. B love is like losing ten pence and finding a fiver. You feel richer, not poorer; more viable as a person, able to do more things, altruistic, generous, out-going. You may also have an inclination to whistle, or to say hello to strangers, to say what you feel and be spontaneous.

With D love, you don't feel better. After a while, you feel awful, as though you've lost your self-image, your love-worthiness, your identity. Some people, after years of D love (and having been told that love is terrific) wonder what is wrong, like Meg. Other people, given the choice between love and throwing themselves in a thorn bush, would make for the hedge without a moment's hesitation. "Love hurts," they cry. Don't blame love. Love, B love, is giving, not taking—especially taking things you don't really want to take (like Meg did for ten years).

The lesson is clear. I've said this before, but it bears repeating. Make sure you *know* what you want—then *say* what you want—before you commit yourself. Don't settle for second-best to please others (or because you're tired). You'll repent—often, at great leisure—if you get too hazy over this kind of vital, emotional decision. If you know exactly what you want from love, you're halfway home to getting it. If you don't, you will be faced with unfinished emotional business later on; you'll have a mid-life crisis of a very traumatic sort, simply because you'll be desperate to find out what real love is all about as it dawns on you, slowly, that what you have is second-rate. With love, at any age, go for the best, insist on quality; it pays off in the long run.

CASE 2

A male menopause, or how a really reliable father freaked out

First, two questions. *Is there a male menopause?* There is. I had mine at thirty-nine, and very shaking it was (more of that later). The MM can be alarming, frightening, totally confusing—even tragic—for those standing nearby. *At what age does it happen?* At any time between thirty and fifty-five, though I've no doubt that there are men of twenty-eight who've spotted a grey hair, had a glimpse of mortality, and hastened to start up an affair with that nineteen-year-old office receptionist. I'm sure, too, that some men get the MM in their sixties, some never get it at all, and some (poor blighters) get it more than once. I can only tell you about what I know, and I hope we can all learn (though I wonder about this) from the trials and tribulations of others.

James was an ace dad, a DIY man, a man who took his kids ice-skating weekly, had built his own kitchen units and panelled the walls of said kitchen in knotty pine, a man who bought his wife flowers on her birthday *and* took her out to dinner, a man for whom a fuse held no terrors and who could even mend things like broken radios, televisions, and bicycles: in other words, a credit to dads everywhere. If the trumpet had sounded for fathers when James was thirty-five, he'd have been in there, through the Golden Gates, among the Good Guys, with no trouble at all. It was the following year that confused the score.

James worked in a small electronics firm and so did Sheila, a young woman of twenty-two summers with a lively mind and good dress sense. Our hero, for whom Sheila typed letters on Tuesdays and Thursdays, fell head over heels in love with her. "It was amazing," he told me. It was. He sent her flowers, wrote poetry to her, frequently bought her little presents (mostly animals in glass/porcelain/clay rather than perfume/silk scarves/diamond bracelets; inexpensive prezzies but, in his case, effective). She loved him back. "He needs me," she said. I saw them in a restaurant one evening, holding hands, smiling at each other in that silly way that lovers (or children who've just wet their trousers) do.

It lasted a year, and during that time James was just about lost to all the rest of us. Angie, J's wife, moved from anger to despair to confusion. "Grow up," she told him during the angry period. Interesting that—maybe that was what J was trying to do. He and Angie had been childhood sweethearts; neither of them had had any other serious relationships before they met at eighteen, courted for a couple of years, and married. By the age of twenty-two, James was into his father's role. I saw his behaviour—or part of it—as a search for lost youth: a yearning for romance, roses, flowers, poetry that he'd never experienced. When J and A were engaged, I recall, they spent most of the time talking about furniture and how to raise the deposit for their house.

James' daughter, a teenager, wasn't too happy about her father's affair. "He's gone off his trolley," she said to me. "Dad's in love with a wonderful girl," she'd sing around the house. I think the whole thing hurt and confused her just as it confused and frightened James' son, aged eleven, who noticed, among other things, that Sunday afternoon sessions with soccer ball or willow and leather over in the park had gradually faded away as father took to going out alone in the car on Sunday. I told my wife about it. "But he's got two kids," she said, "and Angie's marvellous. What does he want anybody else for? That's one of the nicest families I know." Me, too, but when the male menopause strikes, it pays scant regard to reason.

I suppose, if you wanted to, you could laugh about this sort of thing. It's a bit like having The Student Prince or Isadora Duncan flitting on and off the stage while the rest of the cast is playing in Anton Chekhov's *Three Sisters*. Angie, during her depressed state, was very prone to tears, and—I thought—almost at a point where she might contemplate suicide. She went to the doctor, got her pills, and kept worrying. "I think he has gone mad," she told me. "He rings her up at night, just to hear her voice. It's more than I can bear." Then she'd break down and cry, really cry, sob, moan. I think she blamed herself for the whole thing, but I didn't think she should take any blame for finding herself married to a man who'd taken the romantic lead in a drama based on a desire for a second (or first?) bite at love's fine careless rapture. "Let's hope it's not rupture," said my wife, when I gave her my view. My wife likes Angie a lot.

Is this case typical? you ask. I don't know. I've seen only a limited range of male menopauses, and I can't claim to know the whole spectrum of signs and symptoms. With James—besides the poetry—I observed loss of appetite (at home), insomnia, excitability, excessive interest in appearance, inability to concentrate, lessening interest in his job, his children, his wife. "I'm a very lucky man," he told me one day over a cup of coffee. I could smell his aftershave from the other side of the table. "My existence up to now has been pretty futile," he said. Ah, buster, your spirit is protesting against an unlived life, an unfulfilled yearning, a feeling of incompleteness, of loss. You want more, you want justice, you want what you never had. I can't condone your actions, but neither can I find it in my heart to say that you are wrong, or immature, or wicked. Who knows? Maybe you *are* lucky.

After about eight months the thing cooled down a bit. Angie got less angry, less tearful; James cut down on the pongy bath gels and started taking his son over to the football field; his daughter started talking to him again. Angie's confused, though. He's still seeing Sheila once a week as far as I can make out. "This has been the worst time in my life," said Angie. "Like living with a stranger, a schizophrenic, lying in bed with a man you don't know at all—just thought you did. I'm totally shaken. I don't think I'll ever get over it." You will, Angie. If you stay together, you'll have to. Time is a great healer. This kind of thing lasts about a year, in most cases. In others it carries on, develops, breaks up the marriage.

"What'll happen?" my wife asked me. How the hell do I know? I'm a psychologist, not an astrologer. If Angie plays it cool—doesn't go back to being angry, weepy, accusatory—my guess is that James will stay. Who needs him? you ask. Angie does (I've asked her). Why *shouldn't* she get angry? you ask. She has, I agree, every right to express her emotions, her reactions. I'm just saying that it's better, if the family is to stay together, for the thing not to be made into more of a crisis than it already is. Last time I heard, he was seeing her—the Vision of Youth—once a fortnight and he'd told me that he still loves her but that he loves Angie as well. That's schizoid, to me. That's pathetic, you say. I know. As far as the kids and his wife are concerned (and James is, I must stress, a really intelligent, attractive man, as well as a good father), that's *progress:* they would rather have half of him than lose him altogether.

Analysis of case 2

Read it and weep. What a fool that Angie is, you could argue. She should have hit him with a left, followed by the bedside lamp, then thrown him out. Maybe, but when A loves B and B loves C, it's no good telling A that B is a fool. Anyway, I think that Angie knew that what was happening *was* very powerful, very important to James, and—although she wouldn't have been able to tell you why—I think she knew deep down that the affair would follow its course whatever she did. She was right. James was smitten by something just as real and as common as the measles, the feeling of doors closing in on you, of life passing you by. This is what, I suppose, the menopausal man feels when it dawns on him that he is nearer to death—if he lives the allotted threescore years and ten—than he is away from it. I saw James looking in the mirror, fretting over grey hairs. He's neither the first nor the last person to behave like that.

For a man, the thirties may be the Decade of Reassessment. He knows that some of his youthful dreams are never going to be fulfilled; he sees a road ahead—the job, limited promotion, paying off the mortgage—that promises few of the Walter Mitty fantasies he used to indulge in when he was younger. He knows that he isn't going to be chairman of Multinational Co Inc, with a chauffeur-driven limousine and a beautiful secretary. In fact, he'll be lucky if he gets Old Jonesy's job in ten years' time—especially since that pushy twenty-year-old was last seen having a drink with the boss. The job, the family, the world now seem less than limitless; much of his life is pleasant, but routine. A man may easily be more in need of excitement, more vulnerable to romance than at any time since he was seventeen.

For a woman it's also Reassessment Time. I'm no sexist. What happens to men in their thirties happens to many women. It's the female version of the "male menopause" and it has nothing to do with the ceasing of menses. *That* comes later, its physical effects are variable, and often trivial when compared with the tremendous *psychological* upheaval that takes place in many married women in their thirties who, up to crisis time, have been the female equivalent of James: excellent mothers, dutiful wives, pillars of strength in the local playgroup. Women can look in the mirror, too, and worry about grey hairs.

Where's all this leading to? I suppose the practical point is to avoid these Big Crises, if you can. If you marry someone and grow apart instead of growing together through the good and bad bits, so that eventually you have nothing in common with your partner, you can't really expect to avoid the BC. You have to have a certain amount of love in all this, and avoid unreal expectations. Marriage *is* a tough business; it doesn't give you everything that you're looking for. There are no guarantees of anything. You have to work at it. Before you go on board the *SS Wedlock* you should discuss your partnership—and what you both want from it—as well as the sort of furniture you intend to buy.

The love comes in when you acknowledge that your partner is as dismayed at reaching the nines—29, 39, 49—as you are: so many hopes unfulfilled, expectations unrealised, oppportunities gone. It hurts for both, but when someone you love is in pain you don't abandon them, you love them more. Love comes in when you accept responsibility for yourself, and for others—especially any children that you decide to bring into the world. They're *yours:* not the State's. You have a responsibility towards them, and it's love that makes that responsibility easier to bear.

You have a tremendous responsibility to yourself— if you want to avoid the Big Crisis—to make sure that you have a good self-image (it helps, at crisis time). You can get that good SI from getting out of the house, improving your skills (and I'm thinking of anything from woodwork, to taking an external degree, to becoming a town or county councillor)—despite having children. Another big crisis is when your children leave home. The only way to be prepared for that is to be a real, participating, interesting human being. Other people, especially your children, may tell you how lovely you are, but most of us feel this need to prove it to ourselves. Climb a few mountains, tackle new areas—it's good for your self-respect.

If you have a good self-image you can get through most things all right; if your SI is in tatters (and why rely solely on the family for that self-respect?), you'll end up at fifty thinking that you haven't come up with the goods in any possible way. Whose fault is that? Nobody said you had to be a martyr, Mother Courage, a Nice Lady, Mrs Perfect. Nobody forced you to be a cardboard cut-out.

If you don't get satisfaction from your job (and thousands don't), take up some outside interests or hobbies, acquire different social skills, run a youth club, take handicapped people or senior citizens out for a ride in your car each Sunday. Do something for others less fortunate than yourself. Why not? Those who live by the mirror, by Me, by self-obsession shall die by the mirror, the Me, the pursuit of promotion of the self.

For women (who, like men, may ask, "Have I got as far as I wanted to?" but mean it in an emotional sense), it's very much up to you to create the psychological space you need in your marriage *as you go along.* If you over-invest in your husband's career, your children, your home, there's not much point in saying at the nines (39, 49, 59), "But I didn't want any of that. What have I got from all those years of sacrifice?" I don't know. You created—or are creating—it, you took a hand in it of your own free will, so what's the point in complaining to or blaming others when it's all your own work?

Marriage involves commitment, unselfishness, sacrifice, love. It's extremely demanding—one of life's self-imposed ordeals to prove your own worth to yourself. I think it's a great achievement to last out, get to the end of the story, stay together, work things out, till death do us part. Fewer people will make it the whole way, so let's hear it for those that do: the ones who have fun together, laugh together, cry together, grow old together, suffer many crises together, and still love each other there at the finish, when they sit—limbs like matchsticks, hair quite grey—next to each other at each end of the sofa and think of the times when they were thirty, and young. It's a hell of a battle. To win it, you really must believe in the idea of it. Really believe.

Tips to help you to avoid some of the nastier bits of the road as you make your journey

○ *Go for authenticity.* Authenticity—a feeling of worth—only comes when the self chimes in with the surroundings. It's up to you to *insist*, from the kick-off, on the kind of surroundings (they don't have to be opulent) you need to flourish, not perish.

○ *No see-saw effect.* Develop together; go up (not down) together; encourage your partner to grow, with you, as a real person. This will save the man being threatened later on by a suddenly emergent and aware woman (why shouldn't she be emergent and aware from the *start*, and all along the way?); it will save a woman being swamped by nappies and chocolaty fingers at twenty-nine and, out of despair, running off with the college lecturer/milkman/unemployed potter six years later.

○ *Don't fear reassessment at any age.* At thirty-nine, very unhappy, I packed in my job, started a new career. Why not? Change can be painful. It can also be exhilarating, a life-giving thump to the heart. I never had any regrets about starting again. I—and my family and friends—reckon it was the best thing I ever did (I don't think they much liked the depressed sort of chap I was before). A change, a fresh job, a renewal of the spirit of adventure can bind a partnership closer together. It's hard for a family to be happy if one of the parents is miserable. Do something about it. You'll survive.

○ *For both women and men, friends outside the family circle are vital.* It's common sense, not the crazier reaches of woman's lib, when I say that there are dangers in being a mum—just playing a domestic role—rather than being a person. The more your gratification, your emotional jollies, come from being relied on by husband and children, the more vulnerable you'll be when your children are teenagers and you and your partner start having to look at each other as real people.

○ *Think carefully before you have children.* No stigma should be attached to any woman who decides not to have children. Be quite clear in your own mind that, if you do have them, they involve a tremendous and long-lasting sacrifice of the freedom to live your own life as you want to. Children can also be very rewarding; they bring adults great happiness. It's up to you. Don't have them and then moan about curtailment of freedom, sacrifice, the tremendous responsibility involved. That's the name of the game. Nobody's forcing you to play.

○ *Never marry to solve a personal problem or because you're depressed and fed-up.* Marriage may be the cure for love, but it's no cure for loneliness. Solve your personal problem first, before you get married. Marry for love, out of joy. If you marry for anything else you'll learn—late or soon—the true meaning of depression and loneliness. Find yourself first; bring strength to a marriage.

○ *Right from the start, talk over any problems—including money, your own vulnerability, your fears, your hopes.* Admit (especially if you're a man) that you feel vulnerable, worried, often afraid. Jawing (anything from budgets to period pains to alarm about dandruff to telling him/her how lovely he/she is) works out better than warring. Marriage is a shared enterprise: that means talking about it all, including who pays the rates, who gets out of bed to console a crying baby, and who tidies the house. Don't keep silent and then afterwards (sometimes, years afterwards) yell, "Unfair!"

○ *Be happy as you go along; don't save it up for the future.* Get in the emotional and social needs as you go along the road, tank up, stop at the wayside, look around. There's nothing more tragic than a man in his fifties, blinded by ambition, married to his job, asking, "What's it all about?" Woman or man, you shouldn't ever invest your all either in a job or in marriage. There's a big world out there, parts of it very beautiful; it would be a pity to miss out on many of the important things in life because you have a terrible urge to prove yourself, ie, earn a big salary or try to be the perfect mum. Who's counting? Only you.

○ *Eschew age-obsession, and ageism.* Looking back on my thirties, it was (except for my forties) the happiest decade of my life. It is for many people. My teen years were awful: *there's* a decade that I wouldn't like to go through again. Enjoy it all—all stages, all ages.

○ *Don't resist change.* Change is one of the major factors in modern life. Change, and grow, alongside your partner. You're going to have a much more exciting and enjoyable life if you accept that you never quite become adult, never quite grow old—not inside, anyway. Stay young inside, no matter what the DOB is in your passport. As I was walking up our road a few weeks ago, an old lady stopped me and said (this is true, honestly), "Young man, you have a nice face." I was delighted. It was the "young" I liked. Mind you, I reckon she must have been a hundred and four, if she was a day.

Love is your guiding principle

It was dusk, and I was walking around our local park with Cedric. He walked on ahead to feed the ducks. "Throw the bread *to* them, not at them," I shouted, "and be careful of the mallards. They don't bite but they can give you a nasty suck." He disappeared into the bushes, as I strolled around the lake.

As I came back, Cedric was standing by a litter bin waving his arms about like a bookie at Epsom. "Wha! Grr!" he yelled. "What the hell's going on?" I asked. Between shouts he told me that there was a rat in the litter bin. "You stay here," he said. "Keep waving your arms, and shout. I'll go and get a stick."

About half an hour later (with every passer-by having given me a funny look and a wide berth), it dawned on me that Cedric wasn't coming back. Anyway, I wasn't all *that* interested in doing severe damage to the lowly rodent. I stopped waving my arms about and shouting "Grr", composed myself, and made my way to The Pure Drop. There, standing at the bar, was Cedric. "Was there really a rat in that litter bin?" I asked him. "Are you stupid or something?" he said. Don't believe everything you're told, saith the preacher.

The themes of this book have been men learning about women, women learning about men, you learning about yourself, and you connecting with others. I can't claim to have done these themes justice. Men and women still have a long way to go in learning about each other. You and I may still have some way to go in learning about ourselves. The real enemy's always inside you.

We've seen Cedric, and Jenny, and Carol, and the rest of them pursuing happiness, pursuing their own truths. Truth is a difficult concept. Your truth is not my truth. You have to find your own truth, follow your own heart. There could be as many truths as there are people.

One snag about the idea of a Universal Truth is the uniqueness of our own inner worlds. Immanuel Kant said that we see things not as they are, but as we are. We do construct our own realities. We see what we want to see, or are taught to see. If we enter a room, we all see different things. Cedric will notice the first attractive woman, I'll be looking to see if there are any books, an alcoholic will notice the drinks on the table, you may be entranced with that interesting-looking man in the corner. Who is to say, of all those things which greet our eyes, which is the most important?

Not me. Not with any certainty. I know what's important for me and you must know what is important for you. My guess is that what is important in life is love. If you have to choose a Ruling Principle, I'd say choose LOVE. God is love. When we love we come closest to being like gods, like angels, rather than apes. Love transforms us. For me, it's *very* important.

Ah (you say), but what kind of love? There are many varieties. Good point. The one I'm interested in is the love you give to people without expecting anything back (though you often do get quite a lot back). It has to be distinguished from needy love which arises from our own pathology: an emptiness, a poverty, an abiding sense of incompletion or destruction within us. Gift love is to do with giving, not taking.

Some years ago, I was invited to the retirement of a primary school headmistress, a nun. She was a diminutive figure with a determined, no-nonsense look about her. She had taught for some forty years, most of them at the same school, and had seen the children come and go, taught the parents of the current juvenile seekers of wisdom and truth. When she stood up to give her valedictory address, she was brief and to the point (everyone, up to then, had been very fulsome, and very moving, in their praise of her). "I'd like to thank all the children," she said, "for giving me so much happiness over the years. It's been a great privilege for me to have been with them and to have watched them grow up." I looked at her face. This was goodbye, finish, but there were no tears. She just looked at us all, with her tired, pale but beautiful face, as though she wanted us to be good, as though she were in her room at school telling Mark not to clobber Susan with his ruler, as though she knew something about the real nature of love. Maybe she did.

I have to admit that I place this kind of altruistic love above romantic, passionate love (though I'm keen on that, too). You must love in your own style; I must love in mine: altruistic, romantic, passionate, whatever. But you *must* love, though some love hurts.

I met an old man who was quite well-off, still reasonably fit, an educated man. "Why don't you go abroad, have a holiday?" I asked him. He could afford it: a cruise, anything. He stayed in all day, never went out, his groceries were delivered to the door. His wife had died the year before. "I miss her so much," he said. "I loved her all my life. I never loved anybody else, just her." He started to cry and I held his hand. That's all I could do. They'd been childhood sweethearts, had been married for more than fifty years. What words can describe such sorrow? What can one say in the face of such a sense of loss?

Loss is a theme in all our lives. "I can't live without you," people say to each other. I don't think that's such a good thing to say. We may have to; we may lose them, time may take them away from us. Better to say, "By loving you, living in the knowlege of you, I am *myself* more abundantly." We die: *there's* an irrefutable truth if you want one. We die with the memories of those we loved and the happiness we shared, and our loved ones die with memories of us. We should pay homage to the dead by remembering their love.

Later I told that old man what I thought. If he believed in God, I said, he should thank God for sending him such a marvellous friend with whom to live his life. We had quite a few chats, the old man and I, in his dark, gloomy living room. The old man didn't believe in God, but he went out and stood by his wife's grave and said, "Thank you." I think it was for the gifts. I hope there is a Heaven, just to surprise him, with golden pavements, comfortable benches. It would be great if those two could meet again. He was a very nice old man.

Joy and sadness. We're all into heartbreak. I wish we were equally into joy, gladness, happiness. I sometimes wish I could magic everybody into touching, loving, being tender towards each other, into having a sense of joy at just being alive. When I see my sister, she always says to me—*à propos de rien*—"I love you." That's a very reassuring thing to say to anybody. Perhaps we ought to say it, every day, to the milkman, the butcher, the woman in the paper shop. Think of the consequences (you say, aghast). How sad that love is something that we find so hard to express, something that is confused with sex. Sex is only a part (when it *is* a part) of the majestic human spectrum of love.

Besides being into joy, I'm into excitement, passion. I once saw a teacher in a class with primary school children. He was teaching them French. The children wore different hats, acted out little plays, took roles as a police officer, a shopkeeper, a librarian. It was absolutely great. Everybody was having a marvellous time. The children were learning something, too. "I love teaching," the chap told me afterwards. I can see that, pal. You teach with fun, with passion, as though it meant something to you.

It's the difference between what is and what could be in teaching—and in life—that sometimes makes me want to weep. I feel like stopping people in the street and shouting at them, "It's not about long faces! It's about passion, intensity, *magic!* It was never meant to be miserable. You've been lied to, misled. Live your lives! Be happy." I'd probably get the same reaction telling the lady in the post office, "I want a stamp and, by the way, I love you." People would think that I was crazy, but I doubt whether anything I did could match the insanity of living a drab, miserable, *nothing* existence, year in, year out. Life is to do with suffering; it is also to do with joy.

I'm pleased that Cedric, Jenny, and Carol have all achieved—in descending order—something of a Live-Each-Day philosophy, something of catching the bird of time as it flies, something of a sense of urgency. Cedric's always had it: that's why I like him. He lives each day as though he were going to die tomorrow; sometimes it becomes a shade frenetic, but it is better than not living at all.

When is Cedric going to get away from sex and from his notion of women as a combination of stern nanny/whore? Where does a real live woman—a partner—fit into this? I'll have to get Cedric a rubber woman; I'm sure that one of those would accept his theories. Anyway, whether or not I agree with Cedric's vision, I have to admit that—as usual—he displays tremendous vigour in the pursuit of it. He's intense, in earnest, about life. Maybe that's not so bad.

Jenny's widening her horizons day by day. She's much less willing to accept the second-rate, the unexciting, the trivial. Jenny's had the *Ugh;* now she wants the *Aah.* I'd put money on Jenny, since she's a very determined person. I think she now has a clearer vision of what she wants from life, what sort of person she wants to be, and I think it will take a machine gun to stop her. She's learning to live *now.* It's a bit late, but better late than never.

Carol does worry me. Carol suffers from the Some-Day-My-Prince-Will-Come Syndrome. When he finally arrives—the Magic Helper—he'll take her away from the ashes of life to a far, far more romantic place. That's fine, in fairy tales. In fairy tales you go to the ball in a coach, dance with the prince. In life, you could walk there in the rain and there's no guarantee that anybody will ask to dance with you. Carol lacks vision. Her world is dominated by the boring Arthur, and by the narrow confines of the town hall. She could change all that if she really wanted to.

Carol also lacks administration, intensity, passion. I'm sure she could get herself transferred to Trading Standards, or Leisure and Amenities, or Africa, if she tried. Men would fall at her feet, She'd get what she wanted. She'd gain confidence in herself as a person. If only she'd make some kind of symbolic gesture, do something exciting. I wish she'd go off to Spain for a year, or throw the Sunday lunch at Arthur, or fling herself—body and soul—at somebody not working at the town hall. I hope Carol doesn't end up an old lady who never did the things she wanted to do. I hope *you* don't.

If we do something radical, outlandish, the world doesn't fall in about our ears. A thunderbolt doesn't crash down on us. If your world does come to an end—and if your world is a sombre, dreary, guilt-ridden world—then good riddance to it. All it takes to be alive is practice, confidence, and not being too afraid of making yourself vulnerable. Better vulnerable and alive than safe and half-dead.

Something of the adventurous, daring spirit that we might all, with benefit, inject into ourselves is suggested by a poem which I like enormously. Since it expresses what I feel about the need for emotional zap, for joy in all our lives, I'm going to quote it in full. It's called *At Lunchtime A Story of Love** and it's by Roger McGough.

When the bus stopped suddenly to avoid
damaging a mother and child in the road, the
younglady in the greenhat sitting opposite
was thrown across me, and not being one to
miss an opportunity i started to makelove
with all my body.

At first she resisted saying that it
was tooearly in the morning and toosoon
after breakfast and that anyway she found
me repulsive. But when i explained that
this being a nuclearage, the world was going
to end at lunchtime, she tookoff her
greenhat, put her busticket in her pocket
and joined in the exercise.

The buspeople, and therewere many of
them, were shockedandsurprised and amused-
andannoyed, but when the word got around
that the world was coming to an end at lunchtime, they put their pride in their pockets
with their bustickets and madelove one with
the other. And even the busconductor, being
over, climbed into the cab and struck up
some sort of relationship with the driver.

Thatnight, on the bus coming home,
wewere all alittle embarrassed, especially me
and the younglady in the greenhat, and we
all started to say in different ways howhasty
and foolish we had been. Butthen, always
having been a bitofalad, i stood up and
said it was a pity that the world didn't nearly
end every lunchtime and that we could always
pretend. And then it happened . . .

Quick asa crash we all changed partners
and soon the bus was aquiver with white
mothballbodies doing naughty things.

And the next day
And everyday
In everybus
In everystreet
In everytown
In everycountry

people pretended that the world was coming
to an end at lunchtime. It still hasn't.
Although in a way it has.

The poem—the way I see it—is a metaphor for being alive, being adventurous, not letting your life ebb away down the narrow rivulets of the daily round, the common task. It *doesn't* mean, as I understand it, that you should go to the top of the road, board a bus, jump on the nearest attractive man/woman and cover his/her upturned face with a thousand butterfly kisses. It just means that, once in a while, you should grab life, grab good experiences, live—while you still have the chance—as though the world really were coming to an end at lunchtime, or this evening, or by the end of the week. For us all, sooner or later, it is.

Find out what's right for you and DO IT. Do what you want, springing out of a real sense of who you are, springing out of your own feelings about yourself; otherwise you'll live for ever in a phoney world—be a stranger inside your own body. Trust intuition, follow your heart. Don't offer others a grotesque parody of the person you really are. Be yourself, and let come what may.

We needn't spend our lives seeking constant affirmation concerning our own lovableness. What we should do is start off by loving ourselves, and then learn to give love (Gift Love). Let other people decide whether they love us. If we polish our skills at loving, enhance our own ability to love, there's no way that other people are not going to love us. It's because we lack confidence, search for love (Need Love) so desperately, that we rarely know what to do when love is offered to us. There's a big book of love. Read it all. Don't just turn the pages and glance at the footnotes.

Getting and spending we miss the whole point of life. The point of life is to find ourselves, to be happy. Your road to that point may not be mine. Happiness and truth can be approached from a lot of different directions. To get there, to the point, we must learn to listen to our own hearts; otherwise, among all the confusion and lies, the drum beat of our own uniqueness gets fainter and fainter. We must learn to look; above all, we must learn to listen. Look at the stars at night; look at the sky in the day. Listen to the birds. Listen to your heart.

Last night I went for my constitutional: once round cricket pitch, over to duckpond, round duckpond, to big lake, round big lake, home. On the way back I saw Arthur standing by this litter bin waving his arms and shouting. "Wahoo, *grr,* whoosh!" A little old lady came up to me and said, "It's disgraceful. All these drunks about the place." I went over to Arthur. "What you doin' then, Arth?" I asked, in a bland sort of way. He told me the story. Out with Cedric. Rat in litter bin. Cedric gone for stick. I went home, left him to it, didn't say a word. People have got to learn to look out for themselves. Everyone makes their own life.